OXFORD
UNIVERSITY PRESS

C000120693

Matrix
Computing for 11–14

Alison Page
Diane Levine
Steve Bunce
Areti Bizior

2

01010
00101

OXFORD
UNIVERSITY PRESS

Great Clarendon Street, Oxford, OX2 6DP, United Kingdom

Oxford University Press is a department of the University of Oxford. It furthers the University's objective of excellence in research, scholarship, and education by publishing worldwide. Oxford is a registered trade mark of Oxford University Press in the UK and in certain other countries

© Alison Page, Diane Levine, Steve Bunce, Areti Bizior 2017

The moral rights of the authors have been asserted

First published in 2017

All rights reserved. No part of this publication may be reproduced, stored in a retrieval system, or transmitted, in any form or by any means, without the prior permission in writing of Oxford University Press, or as expressly permitted by law, by licence or under terms agreed with the appropriate reprographics rights organization. Enquiries concerning reproduction outside the scope of the above should be sent to the Rights Department, Oxford University Press, at the address above.

You must not circulate this work in any other form and you must impose this same condition on any acquirer

British Library Cataloguing in Publication Data
Data available

ISBN 9780198395553

1 3 5 7 9 10 8 6 4 2

Paper used in the production of this book is a natural, recyclable product made from wood grown in sustainable forests. The manufacturing process conforms to the environmental regulations of the country of origin.

Printed in China by Golden Cup

Acknowledgements

Thanks to:
Howard Lincoln, Educational Consultant and author, for chapters reviewed.
Dr Dov Stekel, Associate Professor of Integrative Systems Biology, Faculty of Science, University of Nottingham, for contributing ideas.
Chris Eccles, MSc, for technical fact checking.

Cover illustration: Koivo at Good Illustration

The publishers would like to thank the following for permissions to use their photographs:
p30t: Hamilton Richards/Creative Commons; p30l: Hulton Archive / Stringer/Getty; p30m: 2013 - The Boston Globe; p30r: Department of Computer Science/Cornell University; p34: Photodisc/OUP; p90-91: Photodisc/OUP; p90: fStop Images GmbH/Alamy Stock Photo; P91: Science & Society Picture Library/Getty; p118-119: Photodisc/OUP; p119l: Quentin Stafford-Fraser/CC BY-SA 3.0; p146-147: Photodisc/OUP.

All other photography by Shutterstock.

Although we have made every effort to trace and contact all copyright holders before publication this has not been possible in all cases. If notified, the publisher will rectify any errors or omissions at the earliest opportunity.

Links to third party websites are provided by Oxford in good faith and for information only. Oxford disclaims any responsibility for the materials contained in any third party website referenced in this work.

Contents

Introduction

What this book is about

As a student, you need to understand how computers work. Most jobs in the future will need computer skills. Do you want to work in manufacturing, agriculture, fashion or education? What about computing? You might be one step away from creating the Internet's next big thing. Whatever you aim to do with your future, computers are everywhere and you will need to use them in some way.

This book will help you to develop your computer skills, so you can take your place in the world of work. It will help you learn to identify problems and solve them.

Even if you just want to use computers for fun, knowing how they work will help you to use them more creatively.

This book is divided into six chapters.

1 **Computational thinking:** Understanding a problem and thinking of the possible solutions is called computational thinking. Computational thinking teaches you a new way to think about the world by breaking problems down into smaller parts. Engineers, scientists, archaeologists, doctors, and musicians all use computational thinking to solve problems.

2 **Programming with App Inventor:** If you have ever used your phone to play a game, send a message, or listen to music, you have used an app. An app is a set of instructions that make the computer inside your phone carry out a task. You will discover how to write your own apps for mobile phones using a programming language that works over the Internet.

3 **Data and the CPU:** What do the International Space Station and an electric toaster have in common? They both use the same basic computer technology. Today, computers are everywhere. Have you ever wondered how a computer works? You will find out how computers communicate and process information.

4 **Programming with Python:** You will learn to write in the same programming language that the professionals use. Python is a popular programming language that uses text-based commands to do many different tasks. You can use Python for just about anything from creating games to analysing research problems. Scientists and engineers at NASA use Python, and so do animators at Disney.

5 Information technology: You have probably used hardware and software in your everyday life. However, you may not know all the things hardware and software can do. You will learn how computer hardware and software work together. People have created the devices that we use for work and entertainment by understanding how hardware and software work together. Knowledge of information technology can enhance your future opportunities for work and fun.

6 Creative communication: Technology can help you get your ideas across to other people creatively. You will build a website to share information about your favourite subjects. Make your website eye-catching so that people will visit. Many people create websites, but knowing how to design a good one takes knowledge and skill.

Learning by doing

In each chapter, you will learn by doing. The activities are designed to develop and stretch your ability. This is not a book to read while sitting and doing nothing. You will be challenged to write, make, create, discuss and invent.

Each chapter begins with an introduction to the theme. Six lessons follow. As you work through the lessons, you will learn new skills and develop your understanding. There are test questions and review activities at the end of each chapter. Answer the questions and complete the activities to show everything you have learned.

What you will find in each lesson

Each lesson takes four pages of the book. In each lesson you will find these sections:

⌘ **Learn about...** You will learn new facts and ideas about each subject.

⏻ **How to...** You will learn how to do new things and develop new skills.

⊕ **Now you do it...** There will be a chance to complete an activity, using your new skills.

🌐 **If you have time...** There are extension activities for students who work quickly and need extra challenges.

▤ **Test yourself...** There are questions to check your understanding of the topic.

Key words New words are explained in each lesson.

Design a route planner

Overview

Computational thinking is a way of thinking through problems and finding good solutions for them. We can apply the principles of computational thinking to programming and to solving problems in our daily lives.

In this chapter you will use the tools of computational thinking to understand the problem of getting from place to place. You will use search and sort algorithms to design a route planning system.

Learning outcomes

By the end of this chapter you will know how to:

- ↗ use computational thinking to solve problems and explain your thinking to others
- ↗ use pseudocode to show your computational thinking
- ↗ design exhaustive algorithms
- ↗ use insertion and bubble sort algorithms
- ↗ use serial and binary search algorithms
- ↗ write search algorithms as pseudocode
- ↗ use an exhaustive algorithm and a greedy algorithm to find the fastest route.

Sorting items into groups

- Move around the room and choose ten small objects to take back to your table.
- Work with a friend to sort your items into a sequence.
- Now sort the items into groups.
- Why did you put some items in one group and other items in another group?
- What do you notice about the ways you think about sequences and groups?

FACT

Sorting

Computer scientists have been trying to work out the most efficient algorithms for sorting since the 1950s.

Algorithm
Sort algorithm
Pseudocode
Selection
Serial search algorithm
Exhaustive search
Bubble sort
Insertion sort
Search algorithm
Iteration
Greedy algorithm
Binary search algorithm
Abstraction

Learning outcomes

When you have completed this lesson you will be able to:

↗ explain your computational thinking to others

↗ use computational thinking to solve problems.

Learn about...

In this lesson you will review what you already know about the basic tools and constructs we use in computational thinking.

What is computational thinking?

Computational thinking is a problem-solving process. This means it is a set of steps we can take to solve a problem. Computational thinking helps us understand a problem, break it down into smaller parts, work out what is important and find a solution.

Do you remember your computational thinking toolbox?

Your toolbox has computational constructs in it. Constructs are the tools that you use to build algorithms.

What is an algorithm?

An **algorithm** is a set of instructions or rules that we create to carry out a task. We can use algorithms to get computers to carry out tasks. We can use the constructs of sequencing, selection and iteration to design algorithms.

Sequencing is the order of the instructions in an algorithm.

Selection happens when you reach a step in the algorithm where there are two or more possibilities.

Iteration is repeating a step or task in an algorithm or computer program. We use loops to show where repetition happens in a computer program so that we do not need to write out the same instruction many times.

What is decomposition?

You use decomposition to break down a problem into smaller parts. As the parts are smaller, they are easier to manage. You can solve small parts of the problem and then bring these parts together to solve the whole problem.

What is pattern recognition?

Pattern recognition is finding the similarities and differences between items. You can use pattern recognition to find the right algorithms to solve a particular problem.

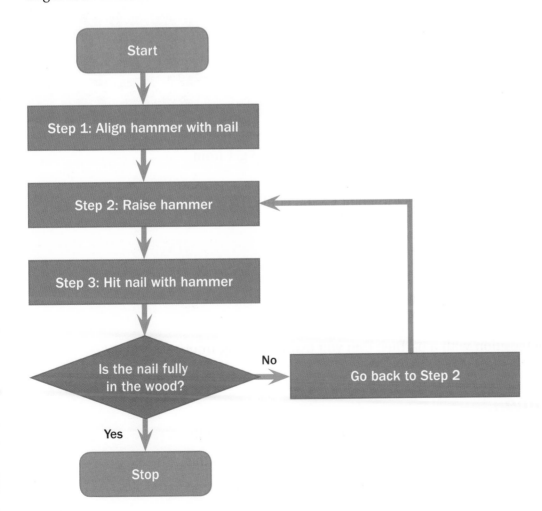

Imagine you are an aeronautical engineer. This means your job is to design aeroplanes. You want to design an aeroplane that flies faster.

You need to decompose the problem to solve it. You might see some patterns. For example, you might look at the way the air flows over different designs of aeroplane wing.

You need to break down the problem and recognise any patterns to find the right solution to the problem.

 How to...

We can use flow charts to show computational thinking.

Imagine you are programming a robot to hammer a nail into a piece of wood.

When you have decomposed the problem you can design a flow chart to show what happens when the robot hammers the nail into a surface. The flow chart might look like this:

Start

Step 1: Align hammer with nail

Step 2: Raise hammer

Step 3: Hit nail with hammer

Is the nail fully in the wood? — No → Go back to Step 2

Yes

Stop

Using iteration, you do not need to write out the same instruction many times. You can simply say that you will repeat (or iterate) particular steps until you tell the algorithm to stop.

Most programmers use the word looping or loop when they talk about iteration. When a program iterates, it loops back to an earlier step.

 ## Now you do it...

In this chapter you will work in a team to design a navigation system.

Start with a simple problem. Imagine you are driving in a car in the city of London. Here is a map of London.

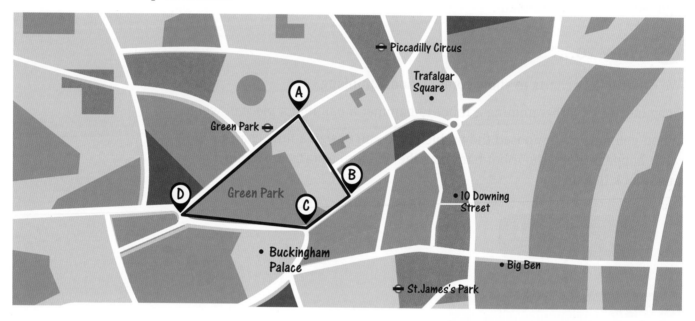

Can you see the dark blue lines? These are the routes you can take to get from point to point on the map. You can move from letter to letter.

You are at point A on the map. You want to get to point C. You could use a route-finding system to help you get from point A to point C.

Decompose your problem by breaking it down into smaller parts.

You can do this by looking at the map.

- ↗ How many points are there on the map?
- ↗ How many routes can you see between point A and point C?
- ↗ Talk about your decomposition with a partner. Can you learn anything from each other?

If you have time...

The green spaces on the map are parks and gardens that you can walk through.

If you walk between point A and point C on the map, instead of drive, does this change the problem?

 Test yourself...

1 What is a loop?

2 A loop is used in which construct or tool?

Create a flow chart of something you do every day, such as brushing your teeth, getting dressed or going to bed.

3 If you have used a loop in your flow chart, draw an arrow to it and label it like this:

←——————————————————————————— loop

4 If you have not used a loop, write a sentence explaining why you do not need a loop in your flow chart.

Key words

Algorithm: An algorithm is a set of instructions or rules that we can use to solve problems or tell a computer what to do.

Iteration: Iteration is repeating a step in an algorithm or computer program.

Selection: Selection is a step in an algorithm where there are two or more possibilities.

Using pseudocode

Learning outcomes

When you have completed this lesson you will be able to:

↗ use pseudocode to show your computational thinking.

⌘ Learn about...

You already know how to use flow charts to show your computational thinking. You also know that you can use programming languages such as Python to write computer programs.

What is pseudocode?

Pseudocode is not a programming language. Pseudocode is meant for us to read, not for computers to follow. Just like a flow chart, pseudocode is a way to:

↗ describe algorithms

↗ show your planning for a program

↗ show how you would solve a problem

↗ show how there might be more than one way to solve a problem.

Unlike flow charts, pseudocode does not use shapes to make diagrams. Pseudocode uses words.

When should we use pseudocode instead of flow charts?

Some people prefer to show their thinking in graphical ways. For these people, flow charts may be better. Other people prefer to show their thinking using words and sentences. For these people, pseudocode may be better.

Flow charts can also be good for working on large projects in groups because everyone can see the whole design.

It is often quicker to write in pseudocode than to draw a flow chart. Pseudocode is a good way of learning to think in computational ways. Computational thinking can help us become good at problem-solving, focusing on problems and finding a general solution to a set of problems.

Using pseudocode is also a good way of learning to write algorithms that are:

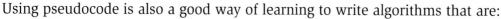

Decomposed

Efficient

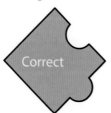
Correct

Elegant

A fit-for-purpose algorithm is:

- ↗ decomposed—the problem has been broken down into smaller parts
- ↗ efficient—the algorithm does the best work for the least effort
- ↗ correct—there are no mistakes
- ↗ elegant—the algorithm is clear, so that someone else can understand it.

 # How to...

Pseudocode and flow charts use similar tools to give instructions, and show selections and iterations.

Look at the flow chart on page 9 that we designed to tell a robot to hammer a nail into a piece of wood.

Writing pseudocode is not like writing a computer program. Programming languages have very clear rules. In pseudocode you can write your instructions in your own way, as long as others can understand it. Most of the pseudocode in this chapter is written in a way that is similar to the rules you are learning in Python.

You could write the flow chart information in pseudocode like this:

```
Align hammer with nail
REPEAT
   Hit nail with hammer
   IF nail fully in wood
      THEN stop
Go back to REPEAT
```

You could write this pseudocode in another way using WHILE.

```
Align hammer with nail
WHILE nail not fully in wood
   Hit nail with hammer
```

This is a more elegant way of writing the algorithm. You are doing the best work for the least effort.

Can you see the loop?

The steps inside the loop are moved to the right compared to the rest of the pseudocode. We say that this text is indented. Indenting the text makes it easier to see which actions are inside the loop.

All of the indented pseudocode shows a block of actions. A block of actions means actions that are always done together.

You could add in an OUTPUT. The robot could show `Job done` once the nail is fully in the wood.

This OUTPUT instruction would look like this in pseudocode:

```
Align hammer with nail
WHILE nail not fully in wood
    Hit nail with hammer
OUTPUT "Job done"
```

It would look like this in the flow chart.

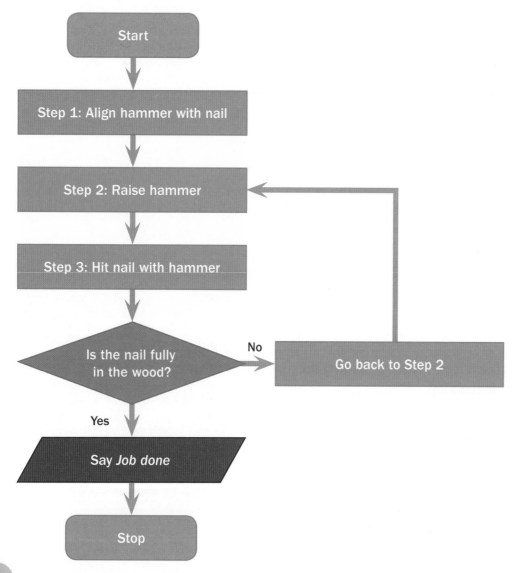

Now you do it...

Do you remember your route navigation problem? You need to get from point A to point C on this map.

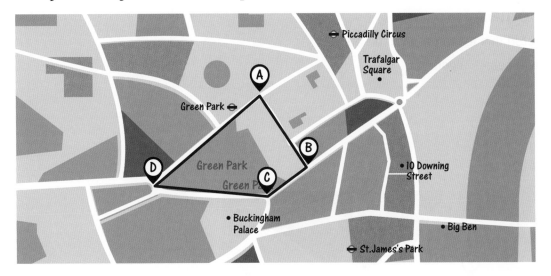

⤴ Write pseudocode to instruct a driver to go from point A, around the route, ending back at point A.

⤴ Remember to use REPEAT or WHILE.

If you have time...

⤴ Work with a partner.

⤴ Discuss whether you prefer to use pseudocode or flow charts and why.

Test yourself...

1 Describe what pseudocode is using your own words.

2 How would you show a loop in pseudocode?

3 Fill in the gap:

Flow charts use diagrams to represent an algorithm. Pseudocode uses .... to represent an algorithm.

4 Create a short algorithm in pseudocode for cutting up an apple.

FACT

Pseudocode

The word pseudocode is made up of two words: pseudo and code. 'Pseudo' comes from a Greek word meaning false or lies. The word pseudo began to be used in English more than 700 years ago. We use pseudo because our pseudocode looks like computer code, but it is not really computer code.

Key words

Pseudocode: Pseudocode is a way to describe algorithms. Using pseudocode can help you show your planning for a program and how you would solve a problem. Pseudocode can also help you see that there might be more than one way to solve a problem. Pseudocode uses words instead of drawings to show your computational thinking.

Learning outcomes

When you have completed this lesson you will be able to:

↗ design an exhaustive search algorithm.

⌘ Learn about...

Do you remember this map?

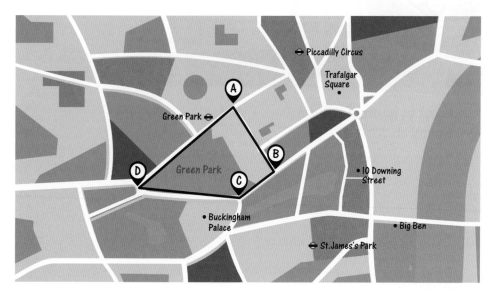

Now you want your route navigation system to find all the possible routes between point A and point C. Your navigation system could use a list like this:

↗ ABC

↗ ADC

There are no more ways you can get from point A to point C.

You can take away any unnecessary detail from the map to help you solve the problem. Your possible routes make a four-sided shape, so you can show our problem as a square. This will help you ignore all of the other details on the map that are not important.

You could show the routes on the map like this:

It is now easier to see all the possible routes. Simplifying a problem in this way is called **abstraction**.

Abstractions

The London Underground map is one of the most famous abstractions in the world. The Underground map shows only the most important information to help people move around London using the underground train system.

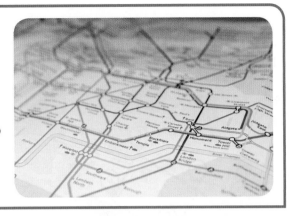

You can make a map that shows more possible routes from point A to point C.

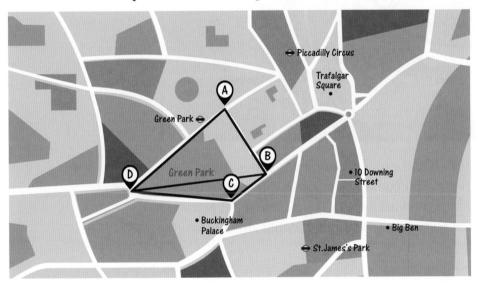

Now you can see there are more possible routes from point A to point C.

Here is a list of every possible route:

- ✈ ABC
- ✈ ADC
- ✈ ADBC
- ✈ ABDC

You can also create an abstraction of the routes on this map:

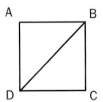

When you explore every possible solution this is called an **exhaustive search.**

⏻ How to...

Now you can use a more complicated map. The previous map had four letters: A, B, C and D. Now the map has six possible points, from A to F. The labels have also changed from the previous map.

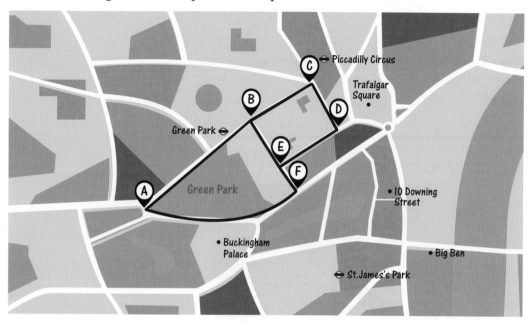

You can also add numbers to your abstraction to show how many minutes it would take to get from point to point. You could use minutes rather than miles or kilometres because there may be road works or traffic to slow you down. Even though two locations may be close to one another, it could still take a long time to get from place to place.

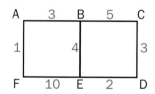

Now you can use an exhaustive search algorithm to work out how long each possible journey might take:

↗ ABC: 3 + 5 = 8 minutes

↗ ABEDC: 3 + 4 + 2 + 3 = 12 minutes

↗ AFEDC: 1 + 10 + 2 + 3 = 16 minutes

↗ AFEBC: 1 + 10 + 4 + 5 = 20 minutes

You can see from this exhaustive search that route ABC is the quickest route.

⊕ Now you do it...

Try using the exhaustive search algorithm to calculate different routes.

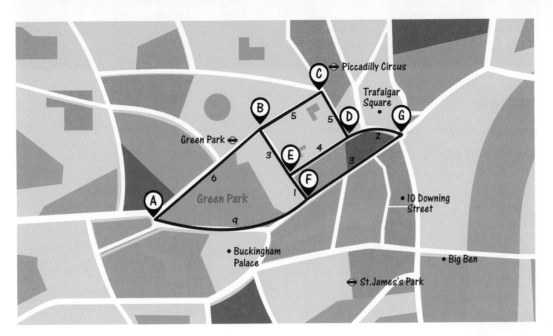

⤴ Work out the exhaustive search algorithm to get from point A to point D.

⤴ Which is the quickest route or routes?

⤴ Which is the slowest route or routes?

⤴ Which routes would take the driver past Buckingham Palace?

🌐 If you have time...

Make a list of the strengths and weaknesses of exhaustive search algorithms.

📄 Test yourself...

1 What is abstraction? Why is it useful in computational thinking?

2 Use this map to create a route with at least three steps. Create an abstraction of the route. Assign each step a number of minutes.

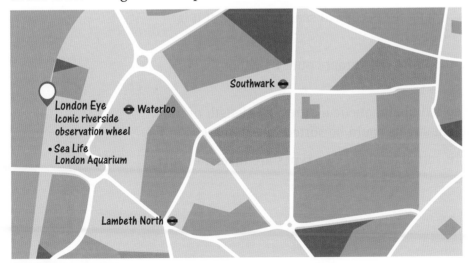

3 Now give your map to a partner. Ask your partner to use an exhaustive search algorithm to get between two points.

4 Check your partner's work. Are your partner's answers correct?

Key words

Abstraction: An abstraction is taking away unnecessary detail to help solve a problem.

Exhaustive search: An exhaustive search algorithm tries every possible solution to find an answer.

Learning outcomes

When you have completed this lesson you will be able to:

↗ use insertion and bubble sort algorithms.

⌘ Learn about...

It is easier to find what you are searching for when your things are organised than when they are not.

It is easy to find the shirt you want in the organised pile

The same is true for computers. A long list is easy to search through if it is sorted into order.

Sort algorithms put a long list into order. The order could be either alphabetical or numerical.

A list of street names could be sorted in alphabetical order. The length of time it takes to travel down the different streets could be sorted into numerical order.

There are many different types of sort algorithm. Two types are **insertion sort** and **bubble sort**.

⏻ How to...

You can learn how to do insertion sorts and bubble sorts.

Do an insertion sort

Here are six famous London landmarks. We are going to sort the names of these landmarks into alphabetical order. We will do this by inserting each name into the correct place. We are going to use the method of insertion sort.

1 Choose the first name: Big Ben.

2 Choose the next name: Tower Bridge. *T* comes after *B* in the alphabet so you will insert it below Big Ben. The list now looks like this:

- Big Ben
- Tower Bridge

3 Choose the next name (Buckingham Palace). *B* is the same as *B*, but *Bu* comes after *Bi* alphabetically. So insert Buckingham Palace in the right place. The list now looks like this:

- Big Ben
- Buckingham Palace
- Tower Bridge

4 Choose the next name on the list (London Eye). *L* comes after *B* but before *T* in the alphabet. So insert London Eye in the right place. The list now looks like this:

- Big Ben
- Buckingham Palace
- London Eye
- Tower Bridge

Can you do the same for the rest of the list?

Insertion sorting is useful if a list is not well sorted at the start of the problem. Insertion sorting is thorough, but it is also expensive. By expensive, we mean that insertion sorting uses a lot of computer processing. Insertion sorting takes time because the computer needs to make a large number of comparisons.

Big Ben

Tower Bridge

Buckingham Palace

London Eye

Trafalgar Square

Tower of London

Do a bubble sort

In a bubble sort the items 'bubble up' to the right place on the list. You can do a bubble sort by comparing two items and swapping them until the items are in the right order. We can do a bubble sort of the London landmarks list:

1   Look at the first two names (Big Ben and Tower Bridge).

2   Are they in the right alphabetical order? Yes. They can remain in the same order.

   - Big Ben
   - Tower Bridge

3   Move on to the next pair on the list (Tower Bridge and Buckingham Palace).

4   Are they in the right alphabetical order? No. Swap them around. Now your list reads:

   - Big Ben
   - Buckingham Palace
   - Tower Bridge

The items in the list bubble up into the right place on the list. Can you do the same for the rest of the list?

The bubble sort algorithm will go through a list again and again until it makes no further changes to the list. That is when the algorithm sees that the list is in the right order.

⊕ Now you do it...

1   Insertion and bubble sorts each have advantages and disadvantages. Work with a partner to copy and complete the table by showing the advantages and disadvantages of each type of algorithm.

	Advantages	Disadvantages
Insertion sort		
Bubble sort		

2   Use a sort algorithm to organise these items into an ordered list. The list can be in numerical or alphabetical order. Use any type of sort algorithm you choose.

   - F to G = 3 minutes
   - E to D = 4 minutes
   - B to C = 5 minutes
   - C to D = 5 minutes
   - F to E = 1 minute
   - A to B = 6 minutes
   - A to F = 9 minutes
   - G to D = 2 minutes
   - B to E = 3 minutes

If you have time...

Insertion and bubble sorts are only two types of sorting algorithm.

1   Research using the Internet to identify two other types of sort algorithms.

2   Write a paragraph describing each algorithm.

 Test yourself...

1   Explain how each of these algorithms work in your own words:
    ● insertion sort   ● bubble sort

2   Why are sort algorithms important in computer science?

3   Look at these six images of a bus. Use an insertion sort to place these buses in order from smallest to largest. Write down the letters as you carry out each step of the algorithm.

a

b

c

d

e

f

4   Use a bubble sort to place these buses in order from largest to smallest. Write the letters as you carry out each step of the algorithm.

Key words

Bubble sort: A bubble sort algorithm compares pairs of items on a list and swaps them into the correct order.

Insertion sort: An insertion sort algorithm puts items into a list one at a time.

Sort algorithm: A sort algorithm puts items into a particular order.

Learning outcomes

When you have completed this lesson you will be able to:

↗ use serial and binary search algorithms

↗ write search algorithms as pseudocode.

⌘ Learn about...

We use **search algorithms** to find a specific piece of information stored in a computer.

Search algorithms

Imagine your navigation system has to find a street in a big city.

Your navigation system would need to search through thousands of street

names to find the right place. Search algorithms save time because they help a computer look through large amounts of information in an efficient way.

There are many different types of search algorithm. Two common types are **serial search** and **binary search**.

How to...

You can learn to do a serial search and a binary search.

Serial search

Now your navigation system has to search for 'Pall Mall', a famous street in London. London has many streets, so there is a long list to search through. You can start a serial search by choosing criteria. Criteria is the plural of the word criterion, which means a rule that must be followed by the algorithm. Criteria are a set of rules.

Every type of search uses criteria, not just serial searches. Criteria are the items that the computer is searching for. The computer could search for more than one criterion. The computer could also find more than one match.

The computer goes through the list, one item at a time. The computer searches for the criterion until it finds a match. In this example there is only one criterion, 'Pall Mall', and you are only searching for one match.

We can show how a serial search works in pseudocode like this:

In this pseudocode we are defining a procedure. We will then tell the computer to run the procedure in different places in the algorithm.

```
DEFINE PROCEDURE serial search ( )
    OUTPUT "Which street name do you need to
    look up?"
    INPUT user inputs Pall Mall
    STORE Pall Mall as street_name variable
    FOR key_name in (list of street names)
        IF street_name equals key_name
            RETURN "match found"
    RETURN "no match found"
```

This loop means create a variable (key_name), and set it to the value of each item in the list in turn.

RETURN ends the procedure. It gives an OUTPUT at the same time.

If the computer reaches this point, it means a match has not been found in the whole list. The computer now ends the procedure.

This pseudocode shows a serial search. The pseudocode starts by asking the name of the street the user is searching for. In this example, the user inputs: Pall Mall.

The algorithm stores Pall Mall as a street name variable. The algorithm then searches through the list of street names in the FOR loop. If it finds Pall Mall it ends with the output "match found". If it does not find Pall Mall anywhere in the list, it ends with the output "no match found".

Serial search is also sometimes called a linear or sequential search.

Binary search

Binary search algorithms are a quick way of searching a sorted list. The list must be sorted, or this type of search will not work.

A binary search works by:

- dividing a list in half
- working out which half the item is in
- repeating the process until the item is found.

⊕ Now you do it...

Serial and binary searches each have advantages and disadvantages. Work with a partner to copy and complete the table by showing the advantages and disadvantages of each type of algorithm.

	Advantages	Disadvantages
Serial search		
Binary search		

In Lesson 1.4 you used a sorting algorithm to sort these routes into an ordered list.

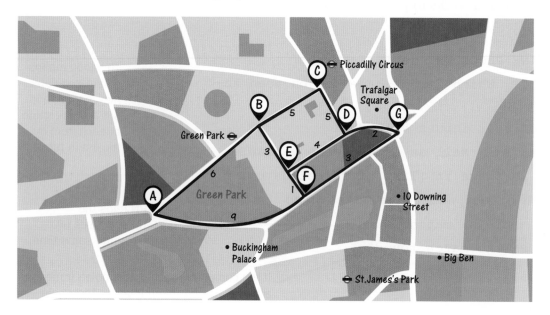

F to G = 3 minutes

A to B = 6 minutes

E to D = 4 minutes

A to F = 9 minutes

B to C = 5 minutes

G to D = 2 minutes

C to D = 5 minutes

B to E = 3 minutes

F to E = 1 minute

Using pseudocode, show how you would use a search algorithm to find the route A to F. You can use any of the search algorithms you know.

If you have time...

Serial and binary searches are only two types of search algorithm. Research using the Internet to find another type of search algorithm and describe it, using your own words.

 Test yourself...

1 What is the difference between a serial search and a binary search?
2 What are the advantages and disadvantages of a serial search?
3 Why are search algorithms important in computer science?
4 When could a search algorithm be useful in a real-life problem?

Key words

Binary search algorithm: A binary search algorithm repeatedly divides an ordered list in half to find an item.

Search algorithm: A search algorithm finds an item with defined characteristics in a list.

Serial search algorithm: A serial search algorithm looks at each item in a list in turn until it finds the item it is looking for.

Learning outcomes

When you have completed this lesson you will be able to:

↗ use a greedy algorithm

↗ compare a greedy algorithm with an exhaustive algorithm.

⌘ Learn about...

You already know about several types of algorithm.

Here are the things you know:

↗ An exhaustive algorithm tries every possible solution to find an answer.

↗ A sort algorithm puts items into a particular order. An insertion sort puts items into a list one at a time. A bubble sort compares pairs of items on a list, and swaps them into the correct order.

↗ A search algorithm finds an item with defined characteristics in a list. A serial search looks at each item in a list in turn until it finds the item it is looking for. A binary search repeatedly divides an ordered list in half to find an item.

You can use computational thinking to help you choose the right kind of algorithm for the problem you are trying to solve.

Sometimes the algorithm that looks like it will be the most efficient or elegant algorithm is not the correct algorithm for the problem. In this lesson you will learn how to compare two algorithms to find the best solution for the problem.

⏻ How to...

In Lesson 1.3 you used an exhaustive algorithm to show all the possible points between point A and point D on this map.

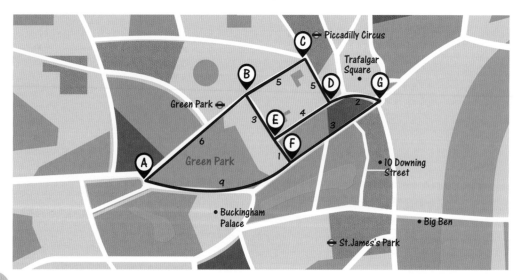

There is another way to find a route between point A and point D. It is called a **greedy algorithm**.

A greedy algorithm looks for simple solutions to complicated problems that have many steps. The algorithm works by choosing which next step will give the most benefit for that part of the problem.

We call these algorithms greedy because, while the best solution for each small step might help for that step, the algorithm does not think about the problem as a whole. The advantage of this algorithm is that it can make the solutions for a small step clear and easy to understand. The disadvantage of this algorithm is that sometimes the best solution to one step in the problem could lead to bad solutions for the problem overall.

In your example, a greedy algorithm would work like this:

Start at point A

AB = 6 minutes

AF = 9 minutes

Choose route AB

Now we are at point B

BC = 5 minutes

BE = 3 minutes

Choose route BE

Now we are at point E

ED = 4 minutes

EF = 1 minute

Choose route EF

Now we are at point F

FG = 3 minutes

Now we are at point G

GD = 2 minutes

Now we are at point D, which is our destination.

Altogether, this route took 15 minutes, and the route went ABEFGD. The algorithm is very simple and seems to be very efficient.

Compare it with the exhaustive algorithm you ran in Lesson 1.3. This gave you the fastest route ABED, which was 13 minutes long.

Which algorithm gives you the fastest route?

⊕ Now you do it...

You have found that the greedy algorithm may not give you the right answer. There is another problem with a greedy algorithm.

Look at this map. Try to work out a route from point A to point C using a greedy algorithm.

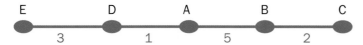

- ↗ Can you work out the route?
- ↗ Now work out the route using an exhaustive algorithm. Can you work out the fastest route?

FACT

Edsger W. Dijkstra

In 1956 a man called Edsger W. Dijkstra invented an algorithm for working out the fastest path between two points. If you are curious about Dijkstra's algorithm, there are many websites you can use to find out more.

🌐 If you have time...

Find out about one of these women in computer science:

Ada Lovelace

Shafi Goldwasser

Eva Tardos

Write five interesting points about the famous computer scientist you have researched and share it with the class.

 **Test yourself...**

For questions 1 and 2, fill in the gaps in the sentences.

1 A serial search algorithm looks at each .... in a .... in turn until it finds the .... it is looking for.

2 A binary search algorithm repeatedly .... a .... list in .... to find an item.

3 Using your own words, write how a greedy algorithm works.

4 Name one strength and one weakness of a greedy algorithm.

Key words

Greedy algorithm: A greedy algorithm looks for simple solutions to complicated problems with many steps. The algorithm works by choosing which next step will give the most benefit for that part of the problem.

Review what you have learned about computational thinking

Overview

In this chapter you used the tools of computational thinking to understand the problem of getting from place to place. You used search and sort algorithms to design a route-finding navigation system.

You have learned how to:

- ✗ use computational thinking to solve problems and explain your thinking to others
- ✗ use pseudocode to show your computational thinking
- ✗ design exhaustive algorithms

- ✗ use insertion and bubble sort algorithms
- ✗ use serial and binary search algorithms
- ✗ write search algorithms as pseudocode
- ✗ use an exhaustive algorithm and a greedy algorithm to find the fastest route.

Test questions

1   You have a number of tools in your computational thinking toolbox. For each of these tools, explain what they are, and why they are important in computational thinking.

   a) pseudocode   **b)** iteration

   c) algorithm   **d)** sequence

   e) selection

2   What is a sort algorithm?

3   What is the name of one type of sort algorithm?

4   What is a search algorithm?

5   What does a binary search do?

6   What is a greedy algorithm?

7   Use a bubble sort to arrange these children in height order from shortest to tallest.

8   Compare the advantages and disadvantages of the two sort algorithms you know about.

9   Compare the advantages and disadvantages of the two search algorithms you know about.

10 What are the strengths and weaknesses of greedy algorithms?

You are designing a computer game set in a castle. In the game, an avatar has to find their way from one room (point A) in the castle to another (point C) using the shortest path. The avatar will need to open a door, move down a passageway and open another door to move from point A to point C.

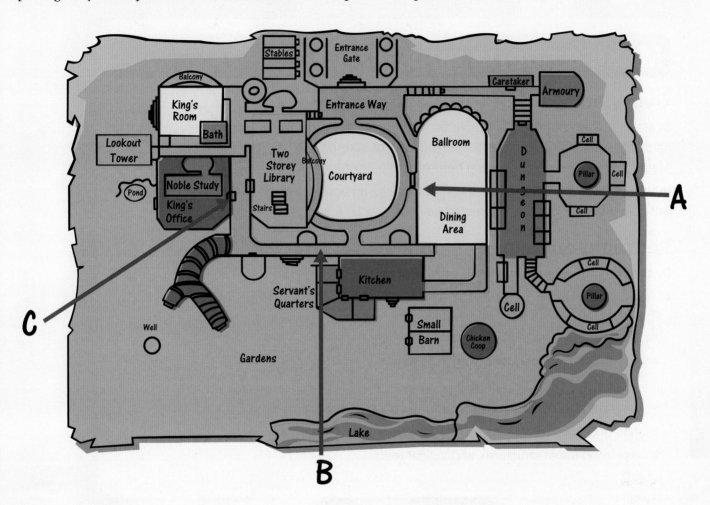

Starter activity

↗ Use pseudocode to show what the avatar will need to do to move from point A to point C.

Intermediate activity

↗ The avatar sees and picks up a casket of treasure at point B on the route. Show this in your pseudocode.

Extension activity

↗ There is more than one door in the passageway. All the doors are locked except the door to point C. Show this in your pseudocode.

↗ If you have time, you could make the doors in the passageway unlocked. What is behind each door? Show what the avatar would encounter behind each door in your pseudocode.

App Inventor

Make a sports app

Overview

In *Matrix 1,* you completed a simple task using App Inventor. You created an electronic ID card that was password protected. If you are not sure how to use App Inventor, look at *Matrix 1,* Chapter 2, App Inventor, before you go any further.

In this chapter you will use App Inventor to make an app for a sports journalist. The app will help a sports journalist to record key facts about a sports event.

Learning outcomes

By the end of this chapter you will know how to:

↗ design an interface to suit users

↗ make an app that records and counts events

↗ use arithmetic operators to change values

↗ initialise, set and get variables

↗ use the real and string data types

↗ find and fix run-time errors

↗ use conditional structures and logical tests.

Design an interface

On paper, design the interface for a mobile app. The interface will help the person who uses the app to record facts during a football match. You can make the interface as complex as you like.

Talk about...

What is your favourite sport? What are the key facts about this sport? What type of data would a reporter need to record when they report on a game or event in this sport?

FACT

Beware American spellings

There are some differences between American and British spelling. App Inventor was made in the USA so it uses American spellings. For example, it uses 'Center' instead of 'Centre'.

Interface Initialise

Syntax error Real number

Global variable **Variable** Run-time error

Local variable

Trigger String **User**

Arithmetic operator

2.1 Make an interface

Learning outcomes

In this chapter you will create a mobile phone app. This app will count goals scored. In this lesson you will create the interface for the app. You will use skills you learned in *Matrix 1*, Chapter 2, App Inventor. Read that chapter again if you need a reminder of how to use App Inventor.

When you have completed this lesson you will be able to:

↗ design an interface to suit users.

⌘ Learn about...

In this chapter you will make an app to count the number of goals at a football match. In this lesson you will make the **interface** for the app.

An interface is used for input and output. A mobile phone has a touchscreen. The screen is used for both input and output.

↗ Input: the screen will have a button for the user to press to count each goal.

↗ Output: the screen will display the number of goals as a label.

The user

The person who will use the app is called the **user**. The programmer must make sure the interface meets the user's needs. The programmer has to think of things like:

↗ what language the user speaks

↗ whether the user has good computer skills

↗ how the user will use the app.

This app will be used at a football match. The user will be busy watching the match. The match will be a crowded and noisy place, so the interface must be clear and bright. The interface must be easy to read.

Object properties

In this lesson you will add objects to the interface. The objects are buttons and labels. You will set the properties of the objects. Properties include colour, text and position. If you choose the right properties you will design a good user interface.

⏻ How to...

Start a new project on App Inventor and find the sections called Palette and Viewer. The Palette includes Layout boxes. You can use a Layout box to help you organise the objects on the interface.

✐ **Click the Layout section of the Palette. Find the box called:**
VerticalArrangement

✐ **Drag the box onto the Viewer**

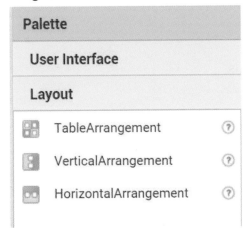

Set properties

Look in the Properties section of the screen. You will set the properties of the
Layout box.

✐ **Click the property: AlignHorizontal**

✐ **Choose Center from the drop-down menu. 'Center' is American spelling.**
App Inventor comes from the USA.

✐ **Click the property Width**

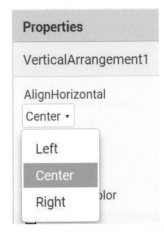

✐ **Select the option Fill parent**

You have changed the width so that the Layout box fills the whole width of
the screen.

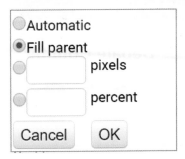

Add objects

You have added a Layout box to the interface.

Remember, the Palette section stores lots of different objects. You can drag objects onto the Viewer. That is how you make the interface.

Now you will add buttons and labels to the interface. The buttons and labels go inside the Layout box.

↗ **Drag two labels onto the Layout box**

↗ **Drag two buttons onto the Layout box**

You have set the alignment of the Layout box to Center. That means the objects will appear in the centre of the box.

Give names to the objects

You have added four objects to the interface.

Now you will set the name and the text property of each object. This table has some suggestions for names and text you might use. If you can't remember how to change the name and text of an object, look back at *Matrix 1*, Chapter 2, App Inventor.

Object	Object Name	Text property
Label1	HeadingLabel	Counter
Label2	Team1Label	0
Button1	Team1Button	Count + 1
Button2	ResetButton	Reset

Design the interface

Now you can design the interface. Make it bright and easy to read. Make changes to label and button properties, such as:

↗ font size, bold, typeface

↗ background and text colours

↗ shape and colour of buttons.

Here is an example of a finished design.

Improve the interface

If you have time you can improve the interface. In *Matrix 1*, Chapter 2, App Inventor, you learned how to upload an image. Use an uploaded image as the background image of the Layout box. This can produce a good interface design.

Perhaps you don't want to make a football app? A student made an app to record a debate. She will press the button when she agrees with a comment. The app will count how many times she agrees.

Another student made an app to record every time a bird landed on her bird table. How would you design this interface?

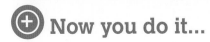 **Now you do it...**

1   Decide what your app will be used for. For example, you might use it for football goals or for debating points.

2   Create an interface for your app.

3   Set the object properties to make the perfect interface design for your users.

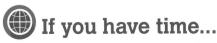 **If you have time...**

At the moment the interface has a count button and a counter label.

When the app is working, the user will press the count button when a goal is scored. The counter label will show the number of goals.

Adapt the interface so there are TWO count buttons and TWO counter labels.

Use these names for the buttons and labels:

↗   `Team1Button`
↗   `Team2Button`
↗   `Team1Label`
↗   `Team2Label`.

Now the interface lets the user make a different goal count for each team in the match. This method will also work to count agreement in a two-person debate.

 Test yourself...

1   An interface is used for two purposes: what are they?
2   Describe the different objects you added to the interface.
3   You changed object properties. What properties did you change?
4   Explain the features that make your interface easy to use.

Key words

Interface: An interface means all the features that let a user work with an app. The interface includes input and output.

User: The user is the person who will use the app. The user inputs data and looks at the output.

Adding up

Learning outcomes

You have created an interface for your app. In this lesson you will add code to the interface. When you click the button on the interface, the counter will count up by one.

When you have completed this lesson you will be able to:

↗ make an app that records and counts events

↗ use arithmetic operators to change values.

⌘ Learn about...

App Inventor is an event-driven programming language. The code you write is always linked to an event. The event is a **trigger**. When the trigger happens, the code is carried out.

Before you start work, think about what the code needs to do. This is called a program plan.

1 The code is triggered when the user touches `Team1Button`

2 The value in `Team1Label` starts at `0`. This number will go up by `1`.

Arithmetic operators

In programming, calculations are carried out by **arithmetic operators.** The main arithmetic operators are:

+ plus

– minus

× multiply

/ divide.

App Inventor uses blocks to make program code. The dark blue Math blocks have arithmetic operators on them. You will use the plus sign in this lesson.

FACT

Math versus Maths

App Inventor was made in the USA so it uses American terms. For example, it uses 'Math' instead of 'Maths'.

⏻ How to...

You are going to add code to your app. Open the Blocks screen. On the left of the Blocks screen is a menu. The coloured squares on the Blocks menu show the main types of block. In this lesson you will use the dark blue Math blocks.

Under the Blocks menu is a list of the objects from Screen1. There are blocks that go with each object. You will use these blocks in your code.

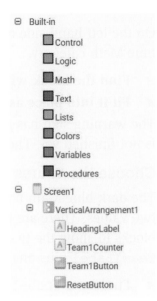

Start making code

At the moment, `Team1Label` shows 0. That is the Text property of `Team1Label`. You set the Text property to 0 when you made the interface.

Remember your program plan.

↗ When the user clicks `Team1Button`, the number in `Team1Label` will increase by 1.

Now you will make code to do that.

↗ **Find** `Team1Button` **in the Blocks menu**
↗ **Select the block which says** `when Team1Button.Click`
↗ **Find** `Team1Label` **in the Blocks menu**
↗ **Select the block which says** `set Team1Label.Text to`

The two blocks fit together like this.

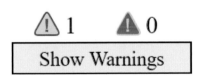

This code means, "When the user clicks `Team1Button`, set the text of `Team1Label` to..."

There is one warning on the screen. The warning tells you there may be a **syntax error** in your program. There is a warning because the code is not finished yet. There is a gap for more blocks to be added.

41

Add one

On the left-hand side of the screen find the dark blue Math category.

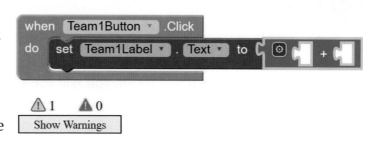

↗ **Find the block with the + (plus) sign**

↗ **Fit it into place as shown**

The warning sign has not disappeared. The code is not finished yet. There are gaps to be filled.

Choose the values

The dark blue Math block with a plus sign is used to add together two values. There are two spaces in the block. You can put in blocks to show the two values. The two values are the number in `Team1Label` plus one.

↗ **Find `Team1Label` on the left-hand side**

↗ **Select the block which says `set Team1Label.Text to`**

↗ **Put this block into the first gap**

↗ **Look in the dark blue Math blocks**

↗ **Find the block with `0` on it**

↗ **Put this block into the second gap and change the value to `1`**

The finished code looks like this:

This code means, "When the user clicks `Team1Button`, add one to `Team1Label`." There are no warning signs because the code has no errors.

Reset button

The job of the Reset button is to return the value of `Team1Label` to `0`. Here is what the code will look like. There is no need to use an arithmetic operator.

⊕ Now you do it...

↗ Make the code to add one to the counter when you click the button.

↗ Run the app to test that it works properly.

🌐 If you have time...

↗ If you have not already done so, extend the interface so it has two buttons and two labels. Call the second label `Team2Label`. See Lesson 2.1 for details.

↗ Now add code to both the buttons on your interface.

Here is a time-saving tip: Make the code for `Team1Button`. Right-click the code block and duplicate it. Use the drop-down menus to change to `Team2Button` and `Team2Label`.

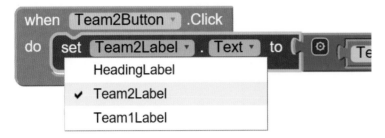

Remember to add code so that the Reset button will set both labels to 0.

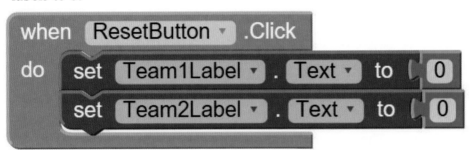

📋 Test yourself...

1 What are the four main arithmetic operators?

2 What is meant by the text property of a label?

3 Clicking `Team1Button` is a trigger. What does 'trigger' mean?

4 Explain what happens in your program when the user clicks each button.

Key words

Arithmetic operator: An arithmetic operator is a symbol that makes the computer carry out a calculation.

Syntax error: A syntax error is a mistake in a computer language. Code with a syntax error cannot run. There is usually a warning message to tell you about syntax errors.

Trigger: A trigger is an event that makes the computer carry out some program code.

Work out the total score

Learning outcomes

You have created an app. The app counts up the goals scored in a football match. In this lesson you will add an extra feature so that your app will count the goals for two teams and add them together to give a total.

When you have completed this lesson you will be able to:

↗ initialise a variable

↗ set the value of a variable

↗ get the value of a variable.

⌘ Learn about...

Program plan

If you have not done so already, you can expand your app so that it counts the goals for two different teams. You can add a new button to the interface. When the user clicks this button:

↗ the computer will add the scores together to give the total match score

↗ the computer will display the total score.

Variables

A **variable** is a location in computer memory. The memory location is given a name. You can `set` the value of the memory location. You can `get` the stored value from the memory location.

Variables can be local or global. What does this mean?

↗ **Local variables** can only be used inside a single block of code.

↗ **Global variables** can be used anywhere in your code.

In this chapter you will use global variables.

Initialise a variable

Making a variable is called declaring or initialising the variable. In App Inventor 'initialize' and 'initializing' are spelled with a 'z'. App Inventor uses American spellings. When you **initialise** a variable you:

↗ choose a name for the variable

↗ choose whether it is a local or global variable

↗ set a starting value for the variable.

In this lesson you will initialise a global variable called `TotalScore`. The variable will store the total match score.

 **How to...**

Prepare the interface

Make sure your interface is set up to record scores for two teams. In Lessons 2.1 and 2.2 this was included as the 'If you have time...' activity. If you have not done these activities yet, your teacher will help you to complete the task.

When you have done this, look at your interface:

↗ **Add a new button to the interface**

↗ **Rename it** `StatsButton`

↗ **Set the Text property to** `Show total`

↗ **Add a new label to the interface**

↗ **Rename the new label** `TotalLabel`

↗ **Set the Text property to** `0`

If you can't remember how to do this, look back at *Matrix 1*, Chapter 2, App Inventor, for help.

In the 'Goal Counter' example you can see we have made the Stats button and the Reset button very wide and set the colours to green and yellow. You can use any design you like.

Variable blocks

Look at the list of blocks. One of the blocks in the list is called Variables. When you select the orange Variables item, you will see these blocks.

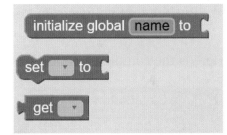

↗ `initialize`: make the variable, give it a name, and set the starting value. Remember that the App Inventor block, `initialize global`, is spelled with a 'z'. App Inventor uses American spellings.

↗ `set`: put a new value into the variable.

↗ `get`: get the value from the variable and use it in the program.

```
initialize global TotalScore to   0
```

Initialise variable

You will make a variable to store the total score. At the start of the match the total is zero.

↗ **Drag the orange** `initialize global` **block onto the Viewer**

↗ **Type the name** `TotalScore` **in the block**

↗ **Add the dark blue Math block** `0`

This code initialises the variable `TotalScore` and sets the starting value to `0`. An initialise block is carried out when you start the app.

set variable

The computer will add the scores for `Team 1` and `Team 2`. The result is the total score. The computer will add the scores when the user clicks `StatsButton`. You will now set the value of the variable `TotalScore`.

↗ **Find the block** `when StatsButton.Click`

↗ **Find the orange** `set` **Variables block and put it inside this block**

If you click the small arrow, you will see a drop-down menu of variables. You have only made one variable so far.

↗ **Choose the variable** `TotalScore`

`TotalScore` is calculated by adding together the scores of `Team1` and `Team2`.

↗ **Find the dark blue Math block with the + operator. The Math block has two gaps.**

↗ **Add it to the** `set` **Variables block**

↗ **Put the text values from** `Team1Label` **and** `Team2Label` **into the gaps as shown**

Here is the completed code block.

get variable

You have `set` the value of `TotalScore`. Now you will `get` the value of `TotalScore`. You will display the value on the interface. You will `set` the text of `TotalLabel`.

↗ **Find the block that sets the Text value of** `TotalLabel`

↗ **Drag this block into the Viewer. The block fits into the code underneath the** `set` **block you just made.**

The code looks like this:

```
when  StatsButton ▾ .Click
do    set  global TotalScore ▾  to  [ ⊙ [ Team1Label ▾ . Text ▾ ] + [ Team2Label ▾ . Text ▾ ]
      set  TotalLabel ▾ . Text ▾  to [
```

This code sets the text value of `TotalLabel`. Now you will set it to display the variable `TotalScore`.

To get the value of the variable you use the `get` block.

↗ **Drag the orange `get` Variables block onto the Viewer**

↗ **Choose the variable name from the drop-down menu**

Here is the complete code you made this lesson:

```
initialize global  TotalScore  to [ 0 ]

when  StatsButton ▾ .Click
do    set  global TotalScore ▾  to  [ ⊙ [ Team1Label ▾ . Text ▾ ] + [ Team2Label ▾ . Text ▾ ]
      set  TotalLabel ▾ . Text ▾  to [ get  global TotalScore ▾ ]
```

You have initialised a variable, and used `set` and `get` to work with the variable.

⊕ Now you do it...

↗ Make all the code to add together the goals scored by the two teams and give the total.

↗ Run the app to check that it works. The app should show the total score of the game by adding the scores of the two teams.

🌐 If you have time...

↗ Add code to the Reset button so that it sets the value of `TotalLabel` to 0.

📄 Test yourself...

1 How would you pick a good name for a variable?
2 What is the difference between a global variable and a local variable?
3 What happens when you initialise a variable?
4 What happens when you set the value of a variable?
5 What happens when you get the value of a variable?

Key words

Global variable: A global variable is a variable that can be used anywhere in your code.

Initialise: Initialise means to create a variable, giving it a name and a starting value.

Local variable: A local variable is a variable that can only be used inside a single block of code.

Variable: A variable is a location in computer memory which is given a name.

2.4 Work out percentages

Learning outcomes

In Lesson 2.3 you made a variable called `TotalScore`. You initialised the variable and used `set` and `get` commands. In this lesson you will extend your app to do more calculations. You will calculate the proportion of goals scored by each team. The app will show this as a percentage.

When you have completed this lesson you will be able to:

↗ use a range of variables in your program code.

 Learn about...

Program plan

The interface has a button with the text `Show Total`. You will change this to `Show Statistics`. When the user clicks this button the computer will:

↗ calculate the percentage score for each team
↗ display these values on the interface.

In this lesson you will practise the skills you have learned so far. You will work with less help.

 How to...

Adapt the interface

You are going to change the interface design. First change the text of `StatsButton`.

↗ **Open the Designer screen**
↗ **Select** `StatsButton`
↗ **Change the Text property to** `Show Stats` (**or** `Show Statistics`)

Now you will add a new section to the interface. This is where the app will show the percentages.

↗ **Add a new horizontal Layout box to the interface**
↗ **Inside this put two labels called** `Stats1Label` **and** `Stats2Label`
↗ **Set the properties of the Layout box and labels to suitable values**

Here is an example of what the finished interface might look like. You use any design you like.

Goal Counter
0
Team 1
0
Team 2
Show Stats
0
Reset
Team 1: Team 2:

Initialise variable

You will create a variable called `Percent1` to store the percentage score for `Team 1`.

- ↗ **Open the Blocks screen**
- ↗ **Use the skills you have learned to initialise a new variable**
- ↗ **The name of the variable is** `Percent1`
- ↗ **The initial value of the variable is** `0`

If you can't remember how to do it, look back at Lesson 2.3.

`set` variable

`Percent1` will show the percentage of all goals that were scored by `Team 1`. Now you will set the value of `Percent1`.

To work out the percentage score of `Team 1`.

- ↗ **Take the score of** `Team 1`
- ↗ **Divide by the total score**
- ↗ **Multiply by** `100`

You will just do the divide part of the sum for now. Here are the blocks you need.

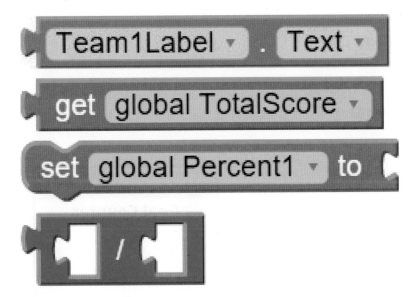

See if you can work out how to fit these blocks together to give the right result.

`get` variables

You have `set` the value of `Percent1`. Now you will `get` that value, and display it in `Stats1Label`.

Here is the completed block.

Assemble the blocks you made

You have made two blocks. The first block sets the value of `Percent1`. The second block gets the value of `Percent1`.

This code is carried out when the user clicks `StatsButton`. So put the blocks inside the `StatsButton` block. The finished code will look like this.

```
when StatsButton .Click
do  set global TotalScore to  [⚙]  ( Team1Label . Text + ( Team2Label . Text )
    set TotalLabel . Text to  get global TotalScore
    set global Percent1 to  ( Team1Label . Text / ( get global TotalScore )
    set Stats1Label . Text to  get global Percent1
```

Complete the code

Now repeat all these commands for `Team 2`.

- ↗ **Initialise a variable called** `Percent2`
- ↗ `set` **the value of** `Percent2` **to** `Team2Label` **divided by** `TotalScore`
- ↗ **Display the value of** `Percent2` **in** `Stats2Label`
- ↗ **Put the blocks inside the** `StatsButton` **block**

Remember, to save time you can.

- ↗ **Duplicate a block**
- ↗ **Change the values using the drop-down menus**

Run the finished program

Run the complete program. The completed app looks something like this.

The two team percentages are correctly calculated, but the display of percentages isn't very good. And if there is no score, the percentage will be shown as `NaN` (not a number). You will do more work to correct these problems in the next two lessons.

 Now you do it...

Use your programming skills to display the team percentages in your example.

 If you have time...

Add code to the `Reset` button so that it clears `Stats1Label` and `Stats2Label`.

 # Test yourself...

Variables can store text as well as numbers. Here is an example of code that uses a text variable.

Now answer these questions about this code sample.

```
initialize global Status to   " Inactive "

when  OnButton ▾ .Click
do    set global Status ▾ to   " Active "
      set ActiveLabel ▾ . Text ▾ to   get global Status ▾
```

1 What is the name of the variable used in this code?
2 What is the value of the variable when the app starts?
3 What is the value of the variable after the user clicks OnButton?
4 How is the value of the variable displayed on the screen?

Text strings

Learning outcomes

You have created an app to count statistics, such as goals at a sports event. The app shows percentages. However, at the moment the output is not as clear as it could be. In this lesson you will use commands that improve the text.

When you have completed this lesson you will be able to:

↗ describe and use real and string data types.

⌘ Learn about...

Data types

In this chapter you have worked with number values. You used whole and decimal numbers. A variable that can store number values, including decimals, is called a **real number** variable (or a 'real' variable for short).

In this lesson you will also work with **string** values. A string is made of text characters. Words, codes, messages and sentences are all strings.

In some programming languages, such as Python, you can't mix up number and string variables. App Inventor is not so strict. In this lesson you will join strings and number values together to make the output of the program.

Make changes to blocks

So far you have made App Inventor programs by fitting blocks together. The blocks are like jigsaw pieces. If you put the blocks the wrong way round they won't join up.

App Inventor blocks aren't exactly like jigsaw pieces, because you can change them. You can add or take away the holes and slots in the blocks. Look out for blocks with a blue cog symbol on them. If you click the blue cog you can make changes to the block.

⏻ How to...

Join text strings

In this lesson you will improve the appearance of `Stats1Label` and `Stats2Label`. At the moment these labels show text like this:

0.25

You will change the text so it looks like this:

Team 1: 25%

To make this improved text the computer will join text strings together. To do this you use the `join` block.

- ↗ **Go to the Blocks screen.**
- ↗ **Look at the pink Text blocks.**
- ↗ **Find the `join` block.**
- ↗ **Drag it onto the Viewer.**

The `join` block lets you join text strings together. The block has two slots. You can join two text strings.

This block has the blue cog symbol on it. That means you can change the shape of this block.

- ↗ **Click the blue cog**

You will see that you add extra slots to the block.

- ↗ **Add an extra text string to the block**

Now the block has three slots.

- ↗ **Use the `join` block to join three strings together:**
  1. **The text string** `Team 1:`
  2. **The value of variable** `Percent1`
  3. **The text string** `%`

Remember, to create a text string you drag an empty pink Text block onto the Viewer. Then you can type in whatever text you want, and fit it into place.

Now the block looks like this.

Multiply by 100

The block still isn't quite right. You need to turn `0.25` into `25%`. To do this you multiply `Percent1` by `100`.

↗ **Use the dark blue Math blocks**

↗ **Multiply** `Percent1` **by** `100`

The block now looks like this.

Now you have made a text block that shows the correct output.

Put the text block in place

In Lesson 2.4 you made a big block of code. The code you made looks something like this.

This code is triggered when the user clicks `StatsButton`. The last two blocks set the value of `Stats1Label` and `Stats2Label`.

↗ **Find the block that sets the value of** `Stats1Label` **to** `Percent1`

↗ **Pull away the block that says** `Percent1`

↗ **Add the pink** `join` **block you just made**

Now make a similar block to replace `Percent2`

↗ **Duplicate the pink** `join` **block**

↗ **Change the values in the new block to** `Team 2` **and** `Percent2`

↗ **Add it to** `Stats2Label`

The completed code will look like this.

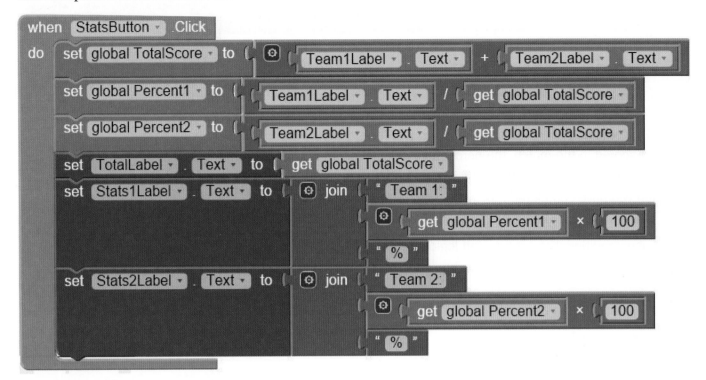

Run the app

When you run the app you should see a display like this. Try it with different goal values.

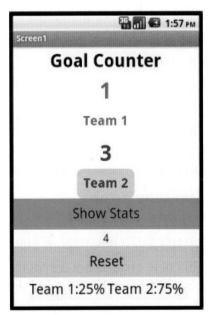

 **Now you do it...**

↗ Complete the coding activity to calculate the percentage of goals scored by each team, or similar percentages, in your example.

↗ Run the app to make sure it works.

 **If you have time...**

In *Matrix 1,* Chapter 2, App Inventor, you learned how to test a program using a range of test data.

↗ Test this app and record the results.

↗ What happens if the score for both teams is 0?

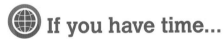 **Test yourself...**

1 What type of data are stored in a real number variable?

2 What is string data?

3 Explain what the pink `join` block does.

4 An App Inventor block has a blue cog symbol, on it. What does that tell you?

Key words

Real number: A real number is a value or variable which can include whole or decimal numbers.

String: A string is a value or variable made of text characters.

55

2.6 Fixing run-time errors

Learning outcomes

You have made a sports app. You can use it to count how many goals are scored in a football match. The app will work out the percentage of the game's total goals scored by each team, but the app has an error in it. If no goals have been scored in the match, the percentage calculation goes wrong. In this lesson you will learn why this error occurs and how to fix it.

When you have completed this lesson you will be able to:

↗ describe a run-time error

↗ use conditional structures and logical tests

↗ fix the run-time error in the program.

 Learn about...

Not a number

Start the app you made. When you start the app, the goal count is 0 for both teams. Click `Show Stats`. You will see an error at the bottom of the screen.

Instead of a percent it says `NaN`. The letters NaN stand for 'not a number'.

The error is shown because the total score is 0. When the computer tries to work out the percent it divides by zero. Dividing by zero is impossible in maths. The result is 'not a number'.

Run-time error

You have learned about syntax errors. Syntax errors are errors that break the rules of a language. If your program has syntax errors it will not run.

This new error is not a syntax error. The new error is a **run-time error**. A run-time error is an error that happens when you run the program. Dividing by zero is a typical cause for a run-time error.

Fixing the error

To fix this error you will use a conditional structure. Remember what you have learned about a conditional structure.

↗ It starts with the word 'if'.

↗ Next there is a logical test.

↗ If the result of the test is "true" then the code is carried out.

You need to test IF the total score is NOT zero. If the total is NOT zero it is OK to calculate the percentage.

 **How to...**

if block

The `if` block is a Control block. The block has the words `if` and `then` on it.

- ↗ **Open the Blocks screen**
- ↗ **Look at the yellow Control blocks**
- ↗ **Drag the `if` block onto the Viewer**

Build the logical test

Now you will make a logical test.

- ↗ **Look at the green Logic blocks**
- ↗ **Drag the logical test block (=) onto the Viewer**
- ↗ **Use the drop-down menu to select the ≠ symbol**

The symbol ≠ means 'NOT equal'.

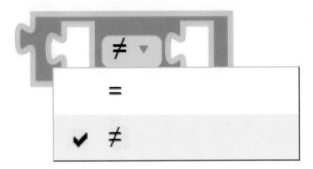

'Not equal' is a logical operator. 'Not equal' checks that two values do NOT match.

This test result is 'true' if `TotalScore` is NOT equal to `0`.

- ↗ **Put blocks in place to make the logical test**
- ↗ **Fit the logical test into the `if` block**

This code means, "If the total score is NOT zero, carry out the actions."

Complete the program

Now you can fit all the blocks together to make the working code.

- ↗ **Pull all the blocks out of the main code (don't delete them, you will need them later)**
- ↗ **Leave behind the first block** (set TotalScore)

The only block you leave behind is the first block, which is the block that calculates TotalScore. You need that first block because TotalScore is used in the logical test.

- ↗ **Put the conditional if block in place**

The code will look like this.

```
when StatsButton .Click
do  set global TotalScore to ( ⊙ ( Team1Label . Text ) + ( Team2Label . Text )
    ⊙ if ( ( get global TotalScore ≠ 0 )
    then
```

You pulled a lot of blocks out of the main code.

- ↗ **Now put all the blocks back**
- ↗ **The blocks fit inside the if block**

The completed code looks like this.

```
when StatsButton .Click
do  set global TotalScore to ( ⊙ ( Team1Label . Text ) + ( Team2Label . Text )
    ⊙ if ( ( get global TotalScore ≠ 0 )
    then set global Percent1 to ( Team1Label . Text / ( get global TotalScore )
         set global Percent2 to ( Team2Label . Text / ( get global TotalScore )
         set TotalLabel . Text to ( get global TotalScore )
         set Stats1Label . Text to ( ⊙ join ( " Team 1: "
                                               ⊙ ( get global Percent1 × 100 )
                                                 " % "
         set Stats2Label . Text to ( ⊙ join ( " Team 2: "
                                               ⊙ ( get global Percent2 × 100 )
                                                 " % "
```

When you run the app there is no run-time error. You have fixed it.

⊕ Now you do it...

↗   Add the conditional structure to fix the run-time error.

↗   Reset the program and run the improved version to check that it works. There is no run-time error.

🌐 If you have time...

↗   Test the app.

↗   Use different test data.

↗   Record the results in a test table.

📄 Test yourself...

1   What does this symbol mean?

$$\neq$$

2   What are the three types of programming error?

3   What is a conditional structure?

4   Explain what error you found in this program and how you fixed it.

Key words

Run-time error: A run-time error is an error which happens when you run a program. Divide by zero is a typical run-time error.

Overview

In this chapter you have learned how to:

- design an interface to suit users
- make an app that records and counts events
- use arithmetic operators to change values
- initialise, set and get variables
- use the real and string data types
- find and fix run-time errors
- use conditional structures and logical tests.

Test questions

1 What does initialise a variable mean?

2 The variables you used in this chapter are all global variables. What does that mean?

3 What is a real number variable?

4 Explain the difference between a syntax error and a run-time error.

5 I want to test that two values are NOT the same. What symbol do I use in the logical test?

Khalid's team at work got a bonus payment. Each person had an equal share. He made an app to work out the share that goes to each person. Answer these questions about his app:

6 He wants to divide the bonus equally between the people in his team. What arithmetic operator should he use?

7 His share is 79.99. What data type is this?

8 He wants to show the value on the screen of the app. What user interface object could he use?

9 If the number of people in the team is set to zero he gets an error. Why is there an error?

10 Explain how he could fix this error.

Assessment activities

The example shown in this chapter counts the number of goals at a football match.

With a few changes you could adapt this app to record other facts. For example, count:

- which team has most passes or most free kicks.

Or you could change the app to use it for a new purpose. You could extend the app to count more than two things. You could change the type of thing that it counts. For example, count:

- results in a Science experiment
- how often different characters speak in a play
- cars, lorries and buses going past your school.

You could add extra statistics such as average and maximum value.

Starter activity

Think of a new app you could make by adapting the sport app. Create an advert for the new app. Your advert should include:

- the name of the new app
- what the interface will look like
- a brief description of its key features.

Make the app sound attractive so people will want to buy it. How much would you charge for this app?

Intermediate activity

- Write a short report on how you could adapt the sports app to a new use.
- Explain what changes you would make to the interface, the code and the format of results.
- What extra statistics might be included in the new app?

Extension activity

- Open the app you made.
- Pick Save project as… from the Projects menu, and save the app using a new name.
- Adapt the app to a new purpose by changing the interface, code and format.

Data and the CPU

Data all around

Overview

This chapter will show you how computers use a number system called binary. You will learn to convert between binary and decimal. You will also perform simple binary addition.

Computers store single items of data in groups of eight binary digits called bytes. Larger amounts of data are measured in units such as kilobytes and gigabytes. You will find out more about these measures and work out how to convert between them.

You will find out how images are stored as binary data. You will also learn how the quality of an image affects its file size.

Learning outcomes

By the end of this chapter you will know how to:

- ↗ write numbers using the binary number system
- ↗ convert between binary and decimal numbers
- ↗ add binary numbers together and count in binary
- ↗ explain the relationship between binary data and file size
- ↗ describe the storage units (for example, kilobyte) that are used to describe computer memory
- ↗ convert between binary storage units such as megabyte and gigabyte
- ↗ describe how images are made up of pixels
- ↗ explain what affects the quality of a picture file
- ↗ explain how picture resolution and colour depth affects file size and quality
- ↗ describe how pixelation can affect pictures.

Talk about...

Do you like listening to music or watching movies? Do you use your phone to take digital pictures? Do you stream music to your phone? We are storing more media these days than we have ever done before.

How large are the data files that we use to store media, such as sound and pictures? How much space do our phones, computers and games consoles need to store media files?

The quality of video games

Early video games used simple pixel characters. Space Invaders and Pac-Man are early examples of video games. In these games, the characters are represented by small, coloured squares. Today we have much more powerful games consoles. The characters can be more life-like, with a higher-quality look and animation than those early video games. Nintendo's Mario is a video game character who began as a simple, low-quality image. Mario now has a high-quality look with smooth animation. These higher-quality images and animations need more data. More data mean we need larger file sizes and greater computer processing power.

Binary

Kilobyte   Megabyte

Binary addition

Pixelation

True colour

RGB colour

Resolution   Gigabyte

Colour depth   Terabyte

Pixel

Carry   **Byte**

Bits, bytes and base 2

Learning outcomes

When you have completed this lesson you will be able to:

↗ write numbers using the binary number system

↗ convert binary numbers to decimal

↗ convert decimal numbers to binary

⌘ Learn about...

In *Matrix 1*, Chapter 3, Data and the CPU, you learned that people and computers use different number systems. We use a number system called decimal. Decimal is also called base 10. Base 10 is a useful term because it reminds us that:

↗ there are ten digits used in the number system (0 to 9)

↗ the value of each digit in a number increases by ten times as you move from right to left through the number.

The computer's microprocessor is a small component made up of millions of tiny electrical switches called transistors. Like any switch, a transistor can only be either on or off. A computer stores and processes data in a simple format because it only understands these two states: on and off. The simple format the computer uses is called **binary**. The binary number system only uses zeros and ones to represent data. Binary is called base 2. Base 2 is a useful term because it reminds us that:

↗ there are two digits used in the number system (0 and 1).

↗ the value of each digit in a number increases by two times as you move from right to left through the number.

Bits and bytes

This is a binary number:

01001101

A binary number only ever contains zeros and ones. Each zero or one in a binary number is called a binary digit. In computing, the term binary digit has been shortened to bit.

A bit is too small to be of practical use to a computer, so computers group bits together. Computers group bits together in the same way we group letters together to make words.

The basic 'word' that a computer uses is eight bits long. Eight bits is called a **byte**. When you write binary numbers, you always write them as full eight-bit bytes, even if that means adding zeros to the start of the number. For example, in binary you would write the decimal number 2 as:

00000010

 **How to...**

In *Matrix 1,* Chapter 3, Data and the CPU, you converted binary numbers into decimal by using a binary number table. Remember:

- ↗ the table has eight columns
- ↗ each column has a header that tells you what a 1 in that column is worth
- ↗ the value of each column increases by two times from right to left
- ↗ the columns that contain zeros can be ignored—they have no value.

To find the answer, add together the values of those columns that contain a 1.

128	64	32	16	8	4	2	1
0	0	1	1	0	0	1	0

The binary number 00110010 is equal to 50 in decimal.

32 + 16 + 2 = 50

- ↗ Draw a copy of the binary number table on a separate sheet of paper.
- ↗ Use the table to convert these binary numbers:
  - • 01101110
  - • 00001101
  - • 11001110
- ↗ Check your answers with a partner.

Converting decimal numbers to binary

Sometimes you will need to convert numbers from decimal into binary. You can use the same binary number table as before to help you. We need to find which column values add up to our decimal number.

128	64	32	16	8	4	2	1

Suppose that you want to convert the decimal number 76 into binary. Here are the rules to follow:

1 Take the decimal value you want to convert, 76.
2 Working from left to right, find the first column heading that is smaller than 76. Write a 1 in that column. In this case, the column is 64.
3 Subtract the 64 from your original number:

76 − 64 = 12

4 Repeat the process from Step 1, using the remainder (12).
5 Keep repeating until you are left with a remainder of 0.
6 When you have finished enter a 0 into any blank columns.

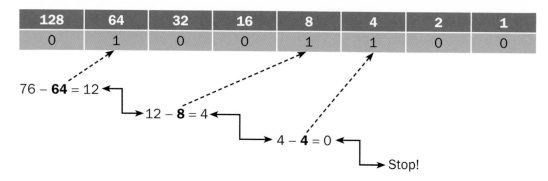

The number 76 in decimal is 01001100 in binary.

1 Draw a copy of the binary number table on a separate sheet of paper.

2 Use the table to convert these decimal numbers into binary:

  • 123   • 201   • 54

3 Check your answers with a partner.

Larger numbers

The largest number that can be stored in a single byte is 11111111. That is 255 in decimal.

If a computer needs to deal with larger numbers it will use groups of bytes joined together. If the computer uses two bytes then the column values are extended across a second byte. You double the value of each column just as you did when using a single byte.

32768	16384	8192	4096	1024	512	256	128	64	32	16	8	4	2	1
Byte two							Byte one							

↗ Two bytes can store numbers up to 65,500.

↗ Three bytes can store numbers up to 16,700,000.

↗ Four bytes can store numbers up to 4,300,000,000!

Storing data

In Chapter 2, App Inventor, you learned that a variable is a location in the computer memory that is given a name. If a program asks you to type your name, the computer stores that information in an area of its memory called a variable. The computer stores your name as binary.

The computer deals with numbers in the same way. If an online shopping app asks you how many items you want to buy, you can enter a decimal number. The computer translates that number and stores it in a variable as binary.

When the computer comes to translate its binary data back into words or numbers, how does it know which is which? The computer must be told which data represents numbers and which represents text. The programmer includes instructions in the program that tell the computer what type of data it is storing. You will learn more about variables in Chapter 4, Introducing Python.

Now you do it...

↗ Copy this table onto a separate sheet of paper.

↗ Complete the table using the methods you have learned for converting between binary and decimal numbers.

Decimal	Binary
93	?
159	?
208	?
?	11011101
?	00010011
?	01001001

 ## If you have time...

Practise recognising short binary numbers without using a pen and paper to convert them. Work with a partner.

1 Cut out 16 equally-sized squares of card or thick paper measuring 10 cm × 10 cm.

2 On one side write the numbers 0 to 15, and on the other, write the binary equivalent in four digits. Write one number per square.

3 Shuffle the cards.

4 Your partner places a card on the table with the binary number facing upwards.

5 Convert the binary number to decimal in your head and call out the answer.

6 Your partner turns the card to reveal if you are correct and moves on to the next card.

7 When you have finished all 16 cards, swap roles with your partner and repeat the game.

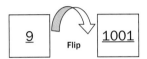

Test yourself...

1 Convert the decimal number 153 into binary.

2 Convert the binary number 01100111 into decimal.

3 What is the largest value (in decimal) that can be stored in a byte?

4 How do computers store large numbers?

FACT

Hexadecimal

Computer scientists do not like using binary. A long string of zeros and ones is hard to read and it is easy to make mistakes. Programmers use another number system in place of binary. It is called hexadecimal. Hexadecimal numbers are one quarter the length of binary. Hexadecimal is also easier than decimal to translate into binary. That is why this number system is popular.

Key words

Binary: The binary (base 2) number system uses two digits (0 and 1). Programmers call these binary digits, or bits. The value of each digit in a number increases by two times as you move from right to left through the number.

Byte: Byte is the basic word that a computer uses. A byte is eight bits long.

Learning outcomes

When you have completed this lesson you will be able to:

↗ add binary numbers together

↗ explain counting in binary.

 Learn about...

In *Matrix 1*, Chapter 3, Data and the CPU, you learned how to count in binary. Counting in either binary or decimal is the same as adding one to a number over and over again. You also learned that a **carry** is a digit that is carried from one column in a number to the next column. This happens when the result of an addition is larger than can be stored in a column. In decimal, the highest column value is 9. In binary, the highest column value is 1.

There are two things that make working in decimal seem easier than binary.

↗ Carrying takes place a lot more often in binary. That is because there are only two digits, zero and one.

↗ Decimal numbers have names: thirteen, fourteen, fifteen and so on. You count and add using these names and don't always think about the maths.

Binary addition

Binary addition is the process of adding binary numbers together. There are just four rules that you need to know when you add two numbers together in binary. If you follow these rules you will be able to add any two binary numbers correctly.

The four rules are:

Rule one: $0 + 0 = 0$		**Rule two:** $0 + 1 = 1$	
0	0 +	0	1 +
0	0	0	0
0	0	0	1
Rule three: $1 + 1 = 10$ (2 in decimal)		**Rule four:** $1 + 1 + 1 = 11$ (3 in decimal)	
0	1 +	0	1 +
0	1	0	1 +
1	0	0	1
		1	1

Remember that you are working in binary. The 10 in Rule three is not 'ten'. Ten is a decimal number. In binary, 10 is pronounced 'one zero' and is the same as 2 in decimal. In Rule four, the 11 is not 'eleven'. In binary, 11 is pronounced 'one one' and is the same as 3 in decimal.

 ## How to...

Here is an example that shows how the four rules can be used to add two binary numbers together. Suppose you want to add together these two binary numbers:

001110 and 011100

To find the correct answer you will have to use all four rules correctly.

You start at the right and add the values in each column, one after the other. Remember to carry according to the rules. Also remember to include any carry when you work out the sum of a column.

Column 1. Rule one: 0 + 0 = 0

Number one	0	0	1	1	1	0	+
Number two	0	1	1	1	0	0	
Sum						0	
Carry							

Column 2. Rule two: 1 + 0 = 1

Number one	0	0	1	1	1	0	+
Number two	0	1	1	1	0	0	
Sum					1	0	
Carry							

Column 3. Rule three: 1 + 1 = 10. The column sum is set to 0 and 1 is carried into the next column.

Number one	0	0	1	1	1	0	+
Number two	0	1	1	1	0	0	
Sum				0	1	0	
Carry			1				

Column 4. Rule four: $1 + 1 + 1 = 11$. You add three 1s as you include the carry from the previous column. The column total is set to 1 and 1 is carried to the next column.

Number one	0	0	1	1	1	0	+
Number two	0	1	1	1	0	0	
Sum			1	0	1	0	
Carry		1	1				

Column 5. Rule three: $1 + 1 = 10$. Always remember to include the carry.

Number one	0	0	1	1	1	0	+
Number two	0	1	1	1	0	0	
Sum		0	1	0	1	0	
Carry	1	1					

Column 6. Rule two: $0 + 1 = 1$.

Number one	0	0	1	1	1	0	+
Number two	0	1	1	1	0	0	
Sum	1	0	1	0	1	0	
Carry	1						

In this example, you:

- took the two binary numbers, 001110 and 011100, and added them together to get the sum, 101010. In decimal, that is $14 + 28 = 42$.
- used the four rules of binary addition
- carried one into the next column when you used Rule three or Rule four
- made sure you used any carry in your column calculations.

Go over the steps again. Make sure you understand what happened at each step before trying your own binary addition. Discuss with a partner if that helps.

⊕ Now you do it...

1   Copy this table onto a separate sheet.

Number one					+
Number two					
Sum					
Carry					

2 Use the four rules to add these two four-digit binary numbers together. Write each of the four steps in the addition. Write the sum of each column and any carry that results from your calculations.

First number: 0011

Second number: 0111

3 When you have finished, convert both binary numbers into decimal. Add the decimal numbers together and check your answer.

4 Make a note of which of the four binary addition rules you used. Were there any you did not have to use in this task?

 ## If you have time...

Carry out the same adding activity but this time add together these two eight-bit bytes:

First number: 10011011

Second number: 00111010

Convert both binary numbers into decimal and add them together. Convert the sum back into binary to check your result.

 ## Test yourself...

1 What is 0 + 0 in binary?

2 What is 1 + 1 in binary?

3 Why does binary addition have a rule for 1 + 1 + 1 if only two numbers are being added together?

4 What happens if you add 00000001 to 11111111 in binary? Can you describe what problem this might cause?

FACT

Binary numbers

Binary mathematics is closely linked to computer science. Binary is the perfect number system for computers, which depend on millions of on-off switches to work.

Modern binary was invented by German mathematician Gottfried Wilhelm Leibniz in 1701. He also invented mechanical calculating machines that were the leading technology at that time.

Leibniz's binary was based on similar number systems that go back to Ancient Egypt and China. Binary was invented a long time before computers.

Key words

Binary addition: Binary addition is adding two or more binary numbers together.

Carry: A carry is a digit that is carried from one column in a number to the next column. This happens when the result of an addition is larger than can be stored in a column. In decimal, the highest column value is 9. In binary, the highest column value is 1.

Learning outcomes

When you have completed this lesson you will be able to:

↗ explain the relationship between binary data and file size

↗ describe the storage units (for example, kilobyte) that are used to describe computer memory

↗ convert between binary storage units, such as megabyte and gigabyte.

 Learn about...

You have learned that a computer stores information in bytes. A byte is made up of eight bits. A byte can hold 256 different values from zero up to 255. In *Matrix 1*, Chapter 3, Data and the CPU, you learned about ASCII code. A computer uses ASCII code to store letters in a code that is made up of binary numbers. Remember that computers can only store and process binary numbers. That is why codes such as ASCII are so important. We would not be able to communicate with computers without codes like ASCII.

In ASCII, a single character takes up one byte of memory. The first paragraph in this section contains over 450 characters, which is about 450 bytes of ASCII code. A paragraph of text is very simple data. A paragraph does not take up much space. Think for a moment about a three-minute music track. How much space would that need in bytes?

A single music track will take up about 4,000,000 bytes. That is four million bytes. You may have several hundred tracks you want to store on your computer. Describing such large chunks of data in bytes means you use very large numbers. You need an easier and more useful way to describe computer memory.

Kilobytes and more

Most countries use the measures kilometre and kilogram. Kilo means one thousand. You might walk three kilometres to school, which is three thousand metres. Two kilograms of apples is two thousand grams.

In computing, one **kilobyte** is 1000 bytes. A byte can hold a single character of text. A kilobyte holds nearly half a page of text. To measure the storage of simple data like text, a kilobyte is a more useful measure than counting in bytes.

New words have been invented to help describe even larger blocks of data. You will probably recognise some of them.

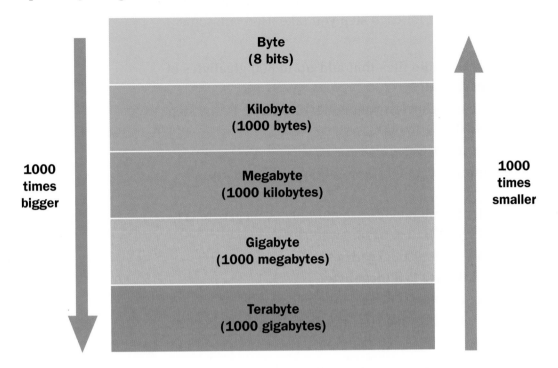

Each time a new measure has been introduced, it is 1000 times greater than the previous measure. A **megabyte** is 1000 kilobytes. A **gigabyte** is 1000 megabytes and a **terabyte** is 1000 gigabytes.

- ↗ A megabyte can hold 500 pages of text.
- ↗ A gigabyte can hold 500,000 pages of text or 350 photos or 250 music files.
- ↗ A terabyte can hold 500 million pages or 350,000 photos or 250,000 music files.

A terabyte is 1,000,000,000,000 bytes, which is one trillion bytes. A terabyte is probably enough space to store all the files of all the teachers and students in your school. Today, many laptops come with a one-terabyte drive installed.

Short names for memory

We use words like megabyte and gigabyte a lot in computing. To save time and space when writing, there are short names that you can use.

Kilobyte	KB
Megabyte	MB
Gigabyte	GB
Terabyte	TB

Sometimes you will see the B left off so that KB becomes K, and so on.

 **How to...**

You can easily convert between the different measures of bytes. You either have to multiply or divide by one thousand for each step you take. Here are some examples.

↗ **Salma has a large number of audio files that add up to 800 gigabytes of data. How many terabytes is that?**

Since terabytes are larger than gigabytes, we divide. A terabyte is one step away from a gigabyte so we divide by 1000:

800 gigabytes ÷ 1000 = 0.8 terabytes.

↗ **Arshad has a folder containing 0.14 terabytes of data. How many megabytes is that?**

Since megabytes are smaller than terabytes, we multiply. A megabyte is two steps away so we multiply by 1000 then again by 1000:

0.14 terabytes × 1000 × 1000 = 140,000 megabytes.

↗ **How much bigger than a kilobyte is a megabyte?**

If you are asked this type of question, you use multiplication:

1 megabyte is 1 kilobyte × 1000. It is one step away so a megabyte is 1000 times larger than a kilobyte.

You can use a calculator to work out the conversions. If you don't have a calculator, remember these rules.

↗ To divide by 1000 move the decimal point three places to the left.

↗ To multiply by 1000 move the decimal point three places to the right.

Work with a partner to try these conversions.

1 How much bigger than a megabyte is a gigabyte?

2 How much bigger than a megabyte is a terabyte?

3 Your teacher has 12 videos she wants to store on the school network. The average size of each file is 4.8 gigabytes. How much space will she use up on the network in terabytes?

Here are some typical file sizes:

e-Book   0.25 MB

MP3 music track   4 MB

Digital photo   3 MB

DVD   4 GB

1 Choose two or three file types. For each, decide on a number of files you want to store. For example, you may wish to store 25 DVDs and 120 MP3 music tracks.

2 Decide on a single storage unit. For example, you might choose terabyte.

3 Work out how much storage space the files you have chosen will take up. Make sure you convert to the storage unit you have chosen.

4 Pass the challenge to your partner. For example, "How many terabytes do I need to store 25 DVDs and 120 MP3 Tracks?"

5 Which one of you can work out the correct solution first?

 ## Now you do it...

Your teacher has set an assignment for one of her advanced classes. Each student has produced a text file. The text files are stored on the school network. All the files are about the same size.

1 An assignment text file contains 2500 words. The average word length is six characters including spaces. How many bytes are there in the file?

2 There are 26 students in the class. How many bytes are in all their files added together?

3 Your teacher wants to take the files home to mark over the weekend. She only has 0.5 megabytes available on her memory stick. Will she be able to fit all 26 files onto the stick?

Hint: You will need to convert the total bytes in the 26 files into megabytes. Then compare the result with the space available on the memory stick. Is the file space needed less than the 0.5 megabytes available?

 ## If you have time...

A Blu-ray disk holds 25 GB of data. How many Blu-ray disks of data could you store on a 1 TB disk drive?

 ## Test yourself...

1 Put these memory units in order from the smallest to the largest:

TB   KB   MB   GB

2 What does kilo mean?

3 How many bytes does it take to store a single ASCII character?

4 How do you convert kilobytes into megabytes?

Key words

Gigabyte: One gigabyte is 1000 megabytes.

Kilobyte: One kilobyte is 1000 bytes. A byte can hold a single character of text. A kilobyte holds half a page of text.

Megabyte: One megabyte is 1000 kilobytes.

Terabyte: One terabyte is 1000 gigabytes.

FACT

How many bytes in a kilobyte?

The kilo in kilobyte means one thousand. In decimal that is written 1000. One thousand in binary is 1111101000. Computer scientists decided that a binary number that used a one followed by zeros would look better. They chose 10000000000. That is 1024 in decimal.

People have argued ever since about whether a kilobyte is 1000 or 1024 bytes. One thousand is now the official measure. The word kibibyte is used for 1024.

3.4 Digital images

Learning outcomes

When you have completed this lesson you will be able to:

↗ describe how images are made up of pixels

↗ explain what affects the quality of an image file.

⌘ Learn about...

In *Matrix 1*, Chapter 3, Data and the CPU, you learned that inside the computer is a microprocessor. This microprocessor is called the central processing unit (CPU). There are many ways to input data into a computer. For example, you can use a keyboard, mouse or touch screen. When you input data, the CPU follows instructions to process that data and produce an output. The computer converts the output data into a form that we can use. For example, you can see the processed data on a computer screen or hear it through speakers.

Inside the CPU, there are many tiny switches that can be on or off. A switch that is 'on' represents a 1. A switch that is 'off' represents a 0. The ones and zeros are binary data. Computers process and transfer all data in binary.

A digital camera also has a microprocessor. When you take a photo using a digital camera or a smart phone, the image is stored as binary data in the internal memory or on a memory card. A digital camera can take photos from low to high quality. The higher the quality of the image, the more data the image contains. So, when the image file is stored, a higher-quality image will have a larger file size than a lower-quality image. The higher-quality image will take up more space on the memory card.

Digital images are made of pixels. A **pixel** is a single point of an image. The pixels are arranged in columns and rows to make up the image. The name pixel comes from the phrase, 'picture element'. Each pixel in an image is represented by a binary number. The binary number stores the colour of the pixel.

⏻ How to...

You can make simple images and shapes using squared paper. Each square shows a pixel. Can you see the shape of the character in the grid? We can call this type of grid pixel art. The grid is eight squares across and eight squares down, so it is an 8 × 8 grid.

To convert this picture to binary, we can say that a white square is a 1 and a black square is a 0.

1	1	0	0	0	0	1	1
1	0	0	0	0	0	0	1
0	0	1	0	0	1	0	0
0	0	0	0	0	0	0	0
0	0	0	0	0	0	0	0
1	1	0	0	0	0	1	1
1	0	0	1	1	0	0	1
0	0	1	1	1	1	0	0

Work with a partner to create your own grids.

1   Draw an 8 × 8 grid like these ones.

2   Create your own design by filling some of the blocks in the grid in black. Leave the others white.

3   Convert each line in your grid into a byte. Each white square is a 1 and each black square is a 0.

   For example, the code for the image used in this lesson is:

   11000011, 10000001, 00100100, 00000000, 00000000, 11000011, 10011001, 00111100

4   Send the binary code to your partner. Can your partner redraw your pattern using the binary code?

How to add more detail to your pixel art

We used an 8 × 8 grid for the image. We used just two colours, black and white. You can make the grid larger and add more colours. By making a 13 × 13 grid, you can add more detail to an image. Also, you can use two binary digits (bits) for each pixel.

In this example, we used 00 for black, 01 for red, 10 for blue and 11 for white.

11	11	00	00	00	11	11	11	00	00	00	11	11
11	00	01	01	01	00	11	00	01	01	01	00	11
00	01	01	01	01	01	00	01	11	11	01	01	00
00	01	01	01	01	01	01	11	10	01	01	01	00
00	01	01	01	01	01	01	11	01	01	01	01	00
00	01	01	01	01	01	01	01	01	01	01	01	00
11	00	01	01	01	01	01	01	01	01	01	00	11
11	11	00	01	01	01	01	01	01	01	00	11	11
11	11	11	00	01	01	01	01	01	00	11	11	11
11	11	11	11	00	01	01	01	00	11	11	11	11
11	11	11	11	11	00	01	00	11	11	11	11	11
11	11	11	11	11	11	00	11	11	11	11	11	11
11	11	11	11	11	11	11	11	11	11	11	11	11

You can code the information in this image in binary, just like we did in the first example. Start at the top left-hand corner. The first and second bytes are:

11110000 and 00111111

If you coded the whole image and sent the code to someone else, they could decode it. To redraw the image, the person receiving the code would use the four pairs of bits in each byte. Each pair of bits is an instruction to use one of the four colours.

The first picture was coded in eight bytes. To code the four-colour heart takes 43 bytes. There are two reasons for the larger number of bytes.

↗ The second picture has more pixels, which means it has a higher resolution. **Resolution** is the number of pixels packed into an image.

↗ The second picture uses more colours which means it has a greater colour depth. **Colour depth** is the number of bits used to show the colour of each pixel.

A higher resolution and a greater colour depth give better quality pictures. Higher resolution and greater colour depth also create larger files.

⊕ Now you do it...

Emojis are the small pictures that are used in text messages. Can you make an emoji using a grid? Use a 15 × 15 grid and 3 colours to create a basic emoji.

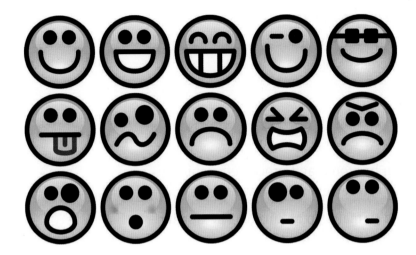

🌐 If you have time...

Use the Kiddle search engine http://kiddle.co/images.php to find images. Search for a smiley face. The results show the images. You can see the size of the pixel grid below each image. If the grid says 200 × 200 for example, that means the image is 200 pixels tall by 200 pixels wide. What is the largest grid you can find? Remember, the larger the grid, the more data the image will contain and the larger the file size.

📄 Test yourself...

1 What are digital images made up of?
2 How many pixels will an image contain if its dimensions are 400 × 200 pixels?
3 How are images stored on a computer?
4 Which contains more data, a high-quality image or a low-quality image?

FACT

Early video games

Early video games contained simple pixel images to show characters. The eight-bit Nintendo Entertainment System had only 54 pixel colours to use and a total screen resolution of 256 × 240 pixels.

Key words

Colour depth: Colour depth is the number of bits used to represent the colour of each pixel in an image.

Pixel: A pixel is a picture element. A pixel is a single point of an image.

Resolution: Resolution is the number of pixels in an image. The higher the resolution of the image, the better the quality of the image. The higher the resolution and quality of the image, the larger the file size.

How computers store true colour

Learning outcomes

When you have completed this lesson you will be able to:

↗ explain picture resolution and how it affects file size

↗ explain how increasing colour depth increases file size.

⌘ Learn about...

In Lesson 3.4 you learned how pictures can be stored and processed as binary numbers. You learned that the quality of a picture depends on two things.

↗ Resolution is the number of pixels used to make up an image. The quality of an image improves if you use more pixels to create it.

↗ Colour depth is the number of bits used to represent the colour of each pixel. Each pixel is a single colour. An image will look more realistic if more colours are used.

In Lesson 3.4 you used a grid of 8 × 8 pixels to create an image in two colours. If you completed the 'If you have time...' activity, you may have found that many emojis are created in a 200 × 200 pixel grid. A 200 × 200 pixel grid contains 40,000 pixels.

If you have a digital camera on your phone it will take digital photos at a resolution of eight megapixels or more. Eight megapixels is 8 million pixels. Photos can create very large files.

It isn't just resolution that makes photo files large. The emojis you found in Lesson 3.4 used between four and eight colours. A digital photo, which is a photo stored as binary digits, can use more than 16 million colours.

Modern computers use three bytes to store colour. This system is called **RGB colour**. RGB stands for Red Green Blue. RGB is also called **true colour**, because the computer can process at least as many colours as the human eye can see.

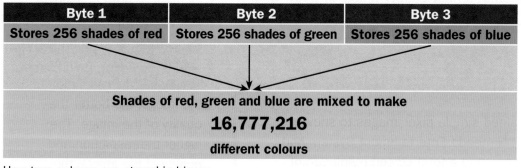

Byte 1	Byte 2	Byte 3
Stores 256 shades of red	Stores 256 shades of green	Stores 256 shades of blue

Shades of red, green and blue are mixed to make

16,777,216

different colours

How true colours are stored in binary

How to...

You can use Microsoft Paint to explore how colour works on a computer.

Open Microsoft Paint. The screen should look something like this image. On the right of the menu ribbon you can see the Edit colours button. Click the Edit colours button.

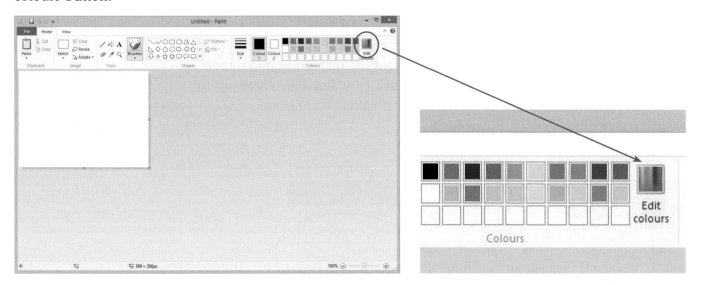

This opens the Edit colours window. Look to the right of the window. You can see three boxes labelled Red, Green and Blue. These boxes help you create a colour by setting the three bytes of the RGB True colour system.

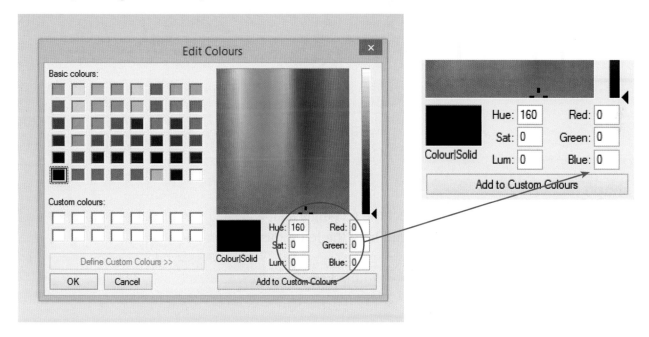

- Notice that all the values are set to 0.
- The colour that these settings make is shown in the box labelled Colour|Solid. If all three bytes are set to 0, the colour made is black.
- You can enter any value in the boxes between 0 and 255.

↗ Every time you change the values, the colour in the Colour|Solid block will change.

↗ Change all the values in the Red, Green and Blue boxes to 255. What happens in the Colour|Solid box?

↗ Enter these values and check again to see what has happened in Colour|Solid: Red = 255, Green = 0, Blue = 0.

↗ Try it again with only Green set at 255. Repeat for Blue.

↗ Mix some colours. Try Red = 255, Green = 255, Blue = 0.

↗ You can now experiment. Try different mixes of colour. You don't have to use 255 and 0. You can use any values between 0 and 255. There are 16 million possible combinations. Try to find a colour you like.

Creating shapes in Microsoft Paint

You can draw a shape and fill it with colour.

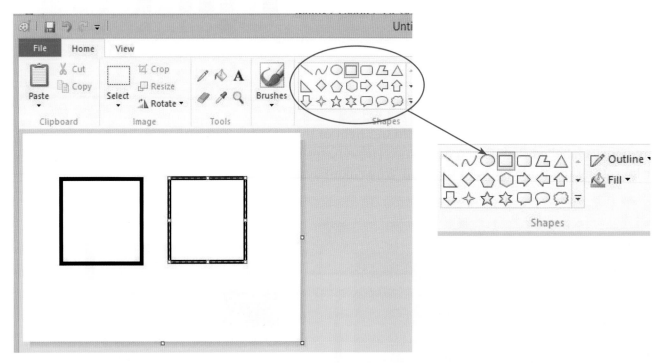

Draw a shape

↗ Find the Shapes menu in the ribbon. Select the rectangle shape.

↗ Move to the Microsoft Paint page. Press and hold the left mouse button and drag to draw a rectangle.

↗ Draw a second rectangle the same size, next to the first.

Fill a shape

↗ Create a colour using the RGB selector.

↗ Click OK. Clicking OK tells Microsoft Paint to use the colour you have just created.

↗ Click the Fill icon in the Tools menu.

↗ Click anywhere inside your shape to fill it with colour.

Practise this with different shapes and colours before you move on.

⊕ Now you do it...

Work with a partner to find out about colour changes.

1 Use Microsoft Paint to set up a new screen. Draw two square boxes close together. Use the RGB colour controls in the Edit Colours window to create a colour of your choice.

2 Fill both boxes with the same colour. Let your partner see the screen.

3 Now ask your partner to look away from the screen.

4 Edit the colour by changing just one of the RGB values by one step. For example, if your original settings were: R = 120, G = 170, B = 30, you might change them to R = 121, G = 170, B = 30

5 Remember to press OK to confirm the change.

6 Use the Fill tool to change the colour ONLY in the right-hand box.

7 Can your partner see a difference between the two colours?

8 If your partner does not see a difference, repeat the process by adding one more to the colour you changed earlier.

9 How many steps does it take before your partner sees the change of colour?

🌐 If you have time...

Repeat the activity. This time, work in groups of four. Do some people see the change more quickly than others?

You can also repeat the activity using a shade of grey as your starting colour. People usually take longer to spot the colour change.

📄 Test yourself...

1 What are the minimum and maximum values (in decimal) that you can set for each of the three colours in the RGB colour system?

2 What colour would you expect to see if these RGB values are set?
R = 0 G = 0 B = 0

3 What are the minimum and maximum values (in binary) that you can set for each of the three colours in the RGB colour system?

4 What colour would you expect to see if these RGB values are set?
R = 150 G = 0 B = 150

FACT

Seeing colours

There are 16 million possible colours in the RGB system. On average, people can only see 10 million of these colours, or about 60 per cent. The other colours are there. We just cannot see the difference between them.

Out of all the millions of colours people can see, most of us can only see around 30 different greys. This is because our eyes are designed to see in colour, not in black and white.

Key words

RGB colour: RGB colour is a method of storing and processing colour on computers. RGB colour uses three bytes to store a colour. One byte is used to store red, one byte is used to store green, and one byte is used to store blue. Red, green and blue are primary colours. This means that all other colours can be made by mixing red, green and blue together.

True colour: True colour is another name for RGB colour. RGB colour can store 16 million colours. That is more than most people can see. For that reason RGB colour can reproduce colour in a realistic way.

Image quality

Learning outcomes

When you have completed this lesson you will be able to:

↗ describe how pixelation can affect images

↗ explain how colour depth affects the quality of an image.

⌘ Learn about...

You have learned that two things affect the quality of images stored on a computer:

↗ resolution

↗ colour depth.

The resolution of a picture is set by the number of pixels that are used to make up the picture. An emoji that you attach to a text message will be made up of a few thousand pixels. If you take a picture on your mobile phone, it will be made up of millions of pixels. Remember that however detailed and realistic a digital image looks, it is still made up of tiny coloured pixels.

You have learned that colour depth affects the number of colours that make up a picture. A photo you take on your phone or digital camera uses three bytes to store the colour information for each pixel.

An emoji will use only one byte or even just half a byte to store the colour information. One byte can only store 256 colours and half a byte can only store 16 colours. Compare that with the 16 million colours that can be stored in three bytes. Using more bytes gives a better quality picture. In this lesson you will see the effect of colour depth on file size.

⏻ How to...

All digital pictures are made up of pixels. If you increase the size of a picture you will eventually see the individual pixels that make up the image. Enlarging an image so you can see the individual pixels is called **pixelation**. To show pixelation, we can open a picture in Microsoft Paint. We will then increase the size of the picture on the screen.

To open a picture in Microsoft Paint, click the File tab and choose Open. Your teacher will tell you where to find the right files.

We have opened a photo of a jug in Microsoft Paint. The jug in the picture looks realistic. Microsoft Paint displays the resolution at the bottom of the screen. In this case the resolution is 1986 × 1489 pixels (px). Nearly three million pixels make up this picture.

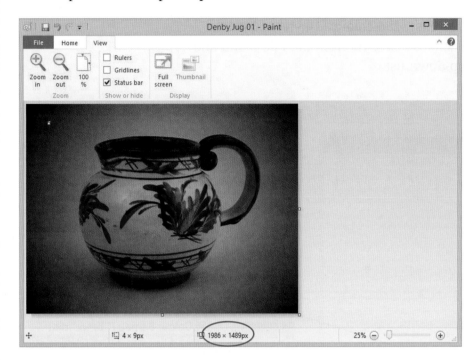

You can use the Zoom in buttons in the View tab to take a closer look at the image. Each click of the Zoom in button increases the size of the picture by 100 per cent. This screenshot shows a detail in the painting magnified by 800 per cent. You can now see the individual pixels. A sloping straight line looks like the edge of a saw. We call this 'saw' effect **pixelation**. Pixelation happens when a digital image is enlarged so that individual pixels can be seen.

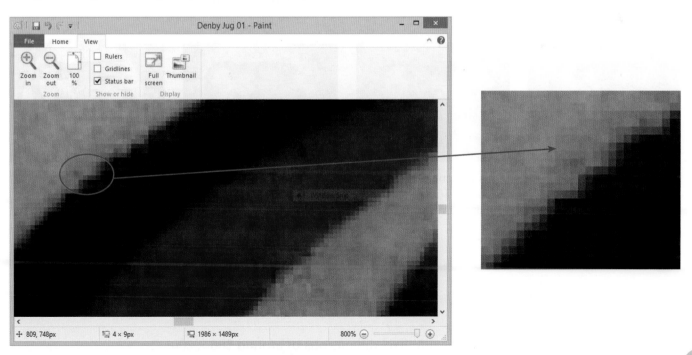

Colour depth

You can use Microsoft Paint to show the effect of colour depth on the quality and the file size of an image.

Using Save As in Microsoft Paint lets you save an image in one of four colour depths: RGB true colour (3 bytes or 24 bits), 256 colour (1 byte), 16 colour (4 bits) and 2 colour (1 bit). You can choose Save As from the File menu and choose one of the options in the drop-down list.

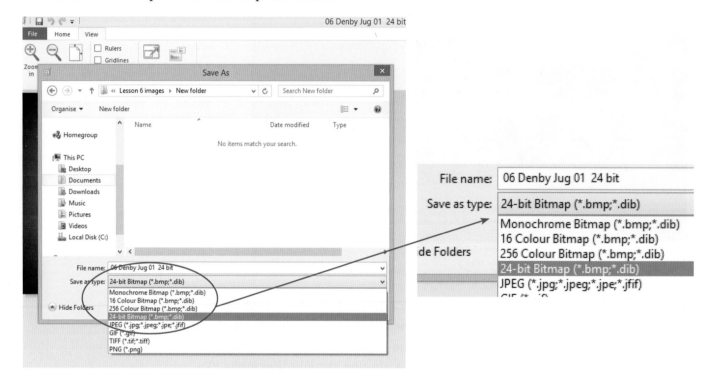

The effect of saving a three-byte (24-bit) as a 256-colour, 16-colour and two-colour image is shown in these pictures. Look at the file sizes of the different pictures.

Bytes per pixel: 3
Colours: 16 million
File size: 8.5 MB

Bytes per pixel:1
Colours: 256
File size: 2MB

Bytes per pixel: 0.5 (4 bits)
Colours: 16
File size: 1.4 MB.

Bytes per pixel: 0.125 (1 bit)
Colours: 2
File size: 366 KB

⊕ Now you do it...

Look at the Kiddle website.

`http://kiddle.co/images.php`

Find an emoji you like. Look for one with pixel dimensions of around 200 × 200.

↗ Download the emoji you choose and open it in Microsoft Paint.

↗ Use the Zoom in tool to magnify the emoji on the screen.

↗ What is the zoom factor when you start to see pixelation? The zoom is shown in the bottom right of the Microsoft Paint window.

↗ Where in the image do you start to see pixelation first?

🌐 If you have time...

↗ Use a picture of yourself or, if you prefer, a picture of a favourite musician or film actor.

↗ Open the picture in Microsoft Paint.

↗ Save the picture in 256-colour, 16-colour and 2-colour monochrome versions. Remember to rename the picture each time you Save As. If you do not rename the picture each time, the original will be overwritten.

↗ How do your results compare with those in the lesson?

📝 Test yourself...

1 Will a high-resolution picture have more pixels than a low-resolution picture?

2 If two versions of the same file were saved in 256-colour and 16-colour format, which would have the larger file size?

3 How many bits are used to save a true colour RGB pixel?

4 How does higher resolution in an image affect file size?

F A C T

Three-byte numbers

The picture of a jug used in this lesson measures 2000 × 1500 pixels. That means the image contains three million pixels. The RGB colour system uses three-byte numbers to store data. A three-byte number looks like this:

111010010100111101010010

That is the data needed to store the colour of one pixel. The three-byte number measures around three centimetres on your page. If all the bytes used to make up the jug were printed out in a line, the line would measure 90 kilometres.

Key words

Pixelation: Pixelation happens when a digital image is enlarged so that you can see the individual pixels.

Review what you have learned about data and the CPU

Overview

In this chapter you have how learned to:

- ↗ write numbers using the binary number system
- ↗ convert between binary and decimal numbers
- ↗ add binary numbers together and count in binary
- ↗ explain the relationship between binary data and file size
- ↗ describe the storage units (for example, kilobyte) that are used to describe computer memory

- ↗ convert between binary storage units such as megabyte and gigabyte
- ↗ describe how images are made up of pixels
- ↗ explain what affects the quality of a picture file
- ↗ explain how picture resolution and colour depth affects file size and quality
- ↗ describe how pixelation can affect pictures.

 ## Test questions

1 Explain the terms bit and byte.
2 Convert the decimal number 156 into a binary byte.
3 Convert the binary byte 01001110 into decimal.
4 Why do computers use binary instead of decimal?
5 How many times bigger than a kilobyte is a gigabyte?
6 Convert 40,500 megabytes into gigabytes.
7 How many colours can be represented in the three-byte RGB colour system?
8 Which two factors change the quality of a digital image?
9 What is a pixel?
10 What is pixelation?

 ## Assessment activities

You can create a video game character by using coloured pixels. Draw the character on squared paper.

Starter activity

Design a video game character.

- ↗ Use a pencil and squared paper to draw a grid of 8 × 8 squares.
- ↗ Shade the squares to create a video game character. For example, you might choose a character similar to Pac-Man.
- ↗ Write a 1 in the squares that are unshaded. Write a 0 in the squares that are shaded.

- Write the numbers for each row on the paper, for example:
  11000011 10000001 00100100 00000000 00000000 11000011 10011001 00111100
- Now send your partner the binary message. Can your partner draw the character you created?

Intermediate activity

Create a second character on a larger grid. Draw a grid of 13 × 13 squares.

- Draw a new character on the 13 × 13 grid using four different colours (black, red, blue and white).
- Label each square using 00 for black, 01 for red, 10 for blue and 11 for white.
- How many bytes are needed to store the data?
- How could you make your character look more realistic?
- Explain how your ideas would increase the file size of your character.

Extension activity

Create a set of instructions to explain how to add two binary numbers together. Someone with no previous knowledge of addition in binary should be able to follow your guide, so make it simple.

Your instructions should:

- Explain the rules to follow when adding in binary.
- Give a step-by-step example showing how two bytes can be added together.
- Give tips on how to check the answer is correct (for example, converting from binary to decimal).

Share your work with a partner. Your partner can tell you if anything is not clear.

4 Introducing Python

The Totaliser

Overview

In this chapter you will use Python to make software for a scientist or other researcher. Researchers collect number data. They process the data to generate key facts. The app you make will allow a user to input numbers and store them as a list. You will process the numbers to work out key facts such as the total and the largest number.

Learning outcomes

By the end of this chapter you will know how to:

↗ calculate values and assign them to variables

↗ select suitable data types, and convert variables to a new data type

↗ use condition-controlled and counter-controlled loops

↗ use arithmetic, relational and Boolean operators

↗ store a sequence of values in a list

↗ find the total value of all the numbers in a list

↗ find the largest number in a list

↗ use validation to help prevent run-time errors.

Talk about...

In this chapter you will make a program to carry out mathematical calculations.

● Do you need to do calculations in your everyday life?

● What subjects at school need calculations?

● Will you need to do calculations in your job when you go into work?

● Do you think students should learn to do calculations without using a computer?

● What are the advantages and disadvantages of using computers and calculators to help us with this type of work?

Make an advert

Think of a job that needs calculations. Make an advert for a computer program that will help people in that job. Your advert should explain the key features of the program—be as inventive as you like.

F|A|C|T

Early calculators

The first calculator was invented by the philosopher Blaise Pascal about 350 years ago. He called it the 'Pascaline'. The calculator didn't use electricity. Pascal invented the calculator to help his father, who was in charge of tax collecting in the French city of Rouen.

In the 19th century, Charles Babbage invented a huge mechanical calculator called the 'difference engine'.

Loop   Iteration

List variable

Item   Function

Data type   Relational operator

Append   Condition-controlled loop

Exit condition   Prompt

Counter-controlled loop   Boolean operator

While loop   Assign a value

Validation   Nested

Initialise a variable

Crash

Learning outcomes

In this chapter you will create a calculator program called The Totaliser. The user will enter a series of numbers. The program will process the numbers, then display statistics such as the total and the average.

In this lesson you will learn about adding numbers together. When you have completed this lesson you will be able to:

↗ calculate values and assign them to variables

↗ select suitable data types

↗ convert variables to a new data type

↗ use arithmetic operators.

⌘ Learn about...

You learned in *Matrix 1*, Chapter 4, Introducing Python, that all data in the computer are held in digital form. The on/off signals inside the computer are used to make binary numbers. All the different types of data must be stored as binary numbers. Here are some examples.

↗ A single on/off signal can be used to store true/false values.

↗ Binary numbers are used to store all types of numerical data.

↗ ASCII code (or Unicode) is a number code that represents letters of the alphabet and other characters.

These different ways of storing data are called **data types**. Every variable has a data type. The data type of a variable restricts what data you can store in that variable. Different programming languages use different names for the data types. This table shows the main data types and what they are called in Python.

Data stored in the variable	Data type	Data type as used in Python
True/False	Logical or Boolean.	boolean
Whole number (no decimal point)	Integer	integer
Number with a decimal point	Real, decimal or 'floating point' numbers.	float
Text values (a string of characters)	Text, character or string data type.	string

Assign a value

A variable is an area of computer memory. A variable can store data. You can **assign a value** to a variable. Assigning a value means you put data into the memory area. You use the equals sign to assign a value to a variable. The general command is like this:

```
variable = value
```

First, you give the name of the variable; then an equals sign, then the value you want to put into the variable.

Initialise a variable

The first time you assign a value to a variable is called **initialising a variable**. Python picks a data type when you initialise the variable. Python picks a data type that matches the assigned value. If you assign letters, Python picks the string data type. If you assign a whole number, Python picks the integer data type, and so on.

There is one exception. If the value of the variable is set by user input, then Python picks the string data type.

Calculation

The value you assign to a variable can be the result of a calculation. The computer does the calculation and then stores the result in the variable. Calculations use the arithmetic operators. Remember, the four most important arithmetic operators used in Python are:

Arithmetic operator	What it does
+	Add together
–	Take away
*	Multiply
/	Divide

You can only use numerical variables in calculations. Other data types, such as string, cannot be used in calculations.

 How to...

You should know how to:

↗ create a Python program
↗ use Python commands, such as `print` and `input`
↗ use variables in Python.

If you don't know how to do this, look at *Matrix 1*, Chapter 4, Introducing Python, to learn about Python.

In this chapter you will make a program called The Totaliser.

↗ **Begin a new Python program**
↗ **Add comments at the top of the program. Note your name and the name of the program**
↗ **Use `print` commands to display the name of the program on the screen**

```
## THE TOTALISER
## Demonstrate Python calculation
## Alison Page

print("=========================")
print("Welcome to THE TOTALISER")
print("=========================")
```

Input to a variable

You will make a program to add two numbers together. You need two variables to store these numbers. In this example we called the variables `number1` and `number2`. You can use any names you like.

The value for the variable will come from user input. Here is the command that assigns user input to a variable.

```
number1 = input("Enter the first number:")
```

The text inside the brackets is the **prompt**. The prompt is a message to the user. The prompt tells the user what to type. You used similar commands in *Matrix 1*, Chapter 4, Introducing Python, to make a multiple choice quiz.

↗ **Add two commands to store user input in two variables**

↗ **Choose suitable names for the variables**

Here are the completed commands.

```
## THE TOTALISER
## Demonstrate Python calculation

print("=========================")
print("Welcome to THE TOTALISER")
print("=========================")
print("This program will add two numbers together")

number1 = input("Enter the first number : ")
number2 = input("Enter the second number: ")
```

Change data type

Python picks the string data type for an input variable. This gives us a problem:

↗ Python always picks the string data type for input

↗ BUT you cannot do calculations with the string data type.

There is a solution to this problem! You can turn a string variable into a numerical variable. Then you can use it for calculations.

This command will convert `number1` to the integer data type.

```
number1 = int(number1)
```

This command will convert `number1` to the float data type.

```
number1 = float(number1)
```

Either data type is suitable. For now you will use the integer data type.

↗ **Add commands to convert the two variables to the integer data type**

Calculate the result

Here is a Python command that adds two variables together. This command uses the arithmetic operator +. The result of the calculation is assigned to a new variable called `answer`.

```
answer = number1 + number2
```

This command prints out the variable called `answer`.

```
print(answer)
```

Here is a better version of the `print` command. It combines different items, separated by commas. That makes the output easier to understand.

```
print(number1, " + ", number2, " = ", answer)
```

↗ **Add commands to calculate and print out the answer**

 Now you do it...

Here is the complete program.

Make this program. Save and run the program.

```
## THE TOTALISER
## Demonstrate Python calculation

print("=========================")
print("Welcome to THE TOTALISER")
print("=========================")
print("This program will add two numbers together")

number1 = input("Enter the first number : ")
number2 = input("Enter the second number: ")

number1 = int(number1)
number2 = int(number2)

answer = number1+number2

print(number1, " + ", number2 , " = ", answer)
```

🌐 If you have time...

1   Change the data type you use in this program from integer to float. Run the program again. What is different?

2   In *Matrix 1*, Chapter 4, Introducing Python, you learned how to test a program. Run tests on the Totaliser program. Record the results of your tests.

📄 Test yourself...

1   What type of data can you store in a Boolean variable?

2   Write the Python command to store user input in a variable called `age`.

3   What data type will Python choose for the variable `age`?

4   You want to add 10 to the value of `age`. What is the problem?

5   What Python command would you use to solve the problem you identified in question 4?

Key words

Assign a value: A variable is a named area of memory. You can assign a value to a variable. When you assign a value, you put that value into the memory area.

Data type: A variable has a data type. A computer stores the different data types in different ways. For example, in Chapter 3 you learned that ASCII and Unicode are used to store text.

Initialise a variable: 'Initial' means 'first'. A variable is initialised when you use it for the first time. Python chooses a data type for the variable based on its initial value.

Prompt: A prompt is a message to the user telling them what value to input.

4.2 Repeat

Learning outcomes

You have created a program that will add up two numbers. In this lesson you will use a loop to repeat the calculation. You will add up ten numbers.

When you have completed this lesson you will be able to:

↗ use a counter-controlled loop

↗ add values together to create a total.

⌘ Learn about...

A **loop** is a program structure. A loop structure contains one or more commands. The commands inside the loop repeat. Each repeat is called an **iteration** of the loop.

Every loop must have an **exit condition**. The exit condition gives you a way to stop the loop from repeating. There needs to be a way to stop the loop or it will go on forever.

Run-time error

In Chapter 2, App Inventor, you learned about run-time errors. A run-time error is a mistake that happens when you run the program. The two most common types of run-time error are:

↗ dividing by zero

↗ an endless loop.

An endless loop will happen if you don't add a proper exit condition to a loop. If your program gets stuck in an endless loop—don't panic! Just close the Python window to stop the program.

Types of loop

There are two main types of loop:

↗ counter-controlled loop

↗ condition-controlled loop.

The two types of loop have different exit conditions.

A **counter-controlled loop** repeats a fixed number of times. The computer counts the number of repeats. When it reaches a set value it will stop. This type of loop is also called a fixed loop. In this lesson you will learn to make a counter-controlled loop.

In Lesson 4.3 you will learn about condition-controlled loops.

⏻ How to...

In this lesson you will make a new Totaliser program. The program will calculate the total of ten numbers. The program will use a counter-controlled loop.

At the start of the program, make a variable called `Total`. At the start of the program this variable has the value 0.

```
Total = 0
```

What data type is this variable?

Counter variable

A counter-controlled loop uses a variable to count the number of iterations. You can call the counter variable any name you like. Some programmers use the name `counter`. That makes sense, but most programmers call the counter variable:

```
i
```

The lower-case `i` is short for iteration. Also, `i` is quick and easy to write.

Start the loop

In Python, a counter-controlled loop is called a `for` loop. A loop that repeats ten times starts like this:

```
for i in range (10):
```

The two dots at the end of the line is a symbol called a 'colon'. A loop that repeats a hundred times looks like this:

```
for i in range (100):
```

What command would you use to make a loop that repeats a million times?

⤴ **Start a loop that repeats 10 times**

Inside the loop

Commands go inside the loop. The commands inside the loop will be repeated. Python indents these commands, which means they are set in from the margin. Python adds the indentation automatically.

These are the commands that should go inside the loop. They are commands you have practised already.

⤴ **Input a value to the variable** number
⤴ **Convert the variable** number **to the integer data type**
⤴ **Add the variable** number **to the variable** Total

Try to make this program using your own skills. The answer is shown on the next page.

After the loop

The final commands in the program are not indented. These lines are not inside the loop. The commands will not be repeated, they will be carried out after the loop has stopped.

➹ **To remove the indentation, press the Delete key. That will stop the indentation.**

➹ **Enter a command to print out the variable** `Total`

Try to make these commands using your own skills. The answer is shown in the 'Now you do it...' below.

 # Now you do it...

Here is the complete program with all the commands you have learned.

```
## THE TOTALISER
## Demonstrate Python loop
## Alison Page

print("========================")
print("Welcome to THE TOTALISER")
print("========================")

print("This program will add 10 numbers together")

Total = 0

for i in range (10):
    number = input("Enter a number : ")
    number = int(number)
    Total   = Total + number

print("the total is: ", Total)
```

1   Enter this code. Correct any errors. Save and run the program.

2   Print out the code and the output to show your achievement.

 # If you have time...

1   At the top of your program add code to:

   • Ask the user how many numbers they want to add

   • Store the input in a variable called `howmany`

2   Change the for loop command from this:

```
for i in range (10):
```

to this:

```
for i in range (howmany):
```

3   Add extra commands at the very end of the program. Divide `Total` by `howmany` to give a new variable called `average`. Print the value of this new variable.

 **Test yourself...**

1   What does exit condition mean?
2   Write the first line of a loop with 23 iterations.
3   What is the data type of the variable `Total` in the program in this lesson?
4   What feature of Python shows you which lines are inside the loop?

Key words

Counter-controlled loop: A loop that repeats a set number of times and then stops is called a counter-controlled loop. A counter-controlled loop is also called a fixed loop.

Exit condition: There must be a way to stop a loop. The way to stop the loop is called an exit condition.

Iteration: Each time a loop repeats is called an iteration.

Loop: A loop is a program structure that repeats one or more commands.

Learning outcomes

You have made a program that adds together exactly ten numbers. In this lesson you will adapt the program so that you can add together as many or as few numbers as you like. You will use a condition-controlled loop.

When you have completed this lesson you will be able to:

↗ use a condition-controlled loop

↗ store a sequence of values

↗ use relational operators.

 Learn about...

In Lesson 4.2 you made a counter-controlled loop. That is a loop that iterates a fixed number of times. In this lesson you will make a **condition-controlled loop**. This type of loop includes a logical test:

↗ every time the loop repeats the computer will do a logical test

↗ when the logical test fails the loop will stop.

You use a condition-controlled loop when you do not want to fix the number of iterations at the start.

The exit condition of the loop is a logical test. The logical test uses a variable. There must be a command inside the loop that lets you change the value of that variable. That is how you can stop the loop.

Types of condition-controlled loop

There are many types of condition-controlled loop in different programming languages. The different types of loop work in different ways.

↗ Some have the test at the top of the loop. Others have the test at the bottom of the loop.

↗ Some stop when the result of the test is 'true'. Others stop when the result of the test is 'false'.

Python has one type of condition-controlled loop, called a **while loop**. A while loop has these features.

↗ The test is at the top of the loop.

↗ The loop stops when the test is false.

You will use a while loop in this lesson.

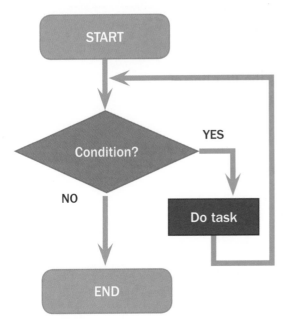

A `while` loop

Relational operators

A logical test normally compares two values. It uses a **relational operator** to compare the two values. Different programming languages use different symbols as the relational operators. This table shows four key relational operators used in Python.

Comparison	Relational operator (Python)
Two values are the same	==
Two values are different	!=
The first value is larger	>
The first value is smaller	<

In Python, a double equals sign means two values are the same.

Can you remember what a single equals sign means?

 **How to...**

You made a program with a counter-controlled loop. Now you will change it to a condition-controlled loop.

In this example you will use a `while` loop. The loop will:

↗ ask the users if they want to add more numbers (answer `Y/N`)

↗ repeat the loop if the answer is `"Y"`

↗ stop the loop if the answer is anything except `"Y"`.

You will need a new variable to store the `Y/N` answer. In this example we have called the new variable `More`, but you can use any name you want. You can use upper-case or lower-case letters, or a mix like we have done, but remember, Python can tell the difference between upper-case letters and lower-case letters. When you have decided what type of letters to use you have to stick with that.

First line of the loop

A `while` loop will repeat if the result of the test is 'true'. Here is the first line of a `while` loop. This loop tests whether the variable `More` holds the value `"Y"`. If that test result is 'true', the loop will repeat.

```
while More == "Y":
```

Remember, the double equals sign means the two values are the same.

- ↗ **Open the program you made**
- ↗ **Change the first line of the loop to this `while` command**

Inside the loop

Every condition-controlled loop uses a logical test as an exit condition. The logical test uses a variable. In this example the variable is called `More`. You need to include a command inside the loop that can change the value of that variable, otherwise there is no way to stop the loop.

This command lets the user input a new value to the variable `More`. This command goes inside the loop.

```
More = input("Do you want to add another number? (Y/N)")
```

The prompt to the users includes `(Y/N)`. That is a message telling them what to type. The prompt helps them enter the right thing.

- ↗ **Add the new input command inside the loop**

Before the loop

Each time the loop repeats, the computer checks whether the variable `More` holds the value `"Y"`. What about the first time the loop starts, though? The variable `More` has no value at that point.

You have to enter an extra line of code right at the top of the program. This code will initialise the variable `More`. The variable will have the starting value `"Y"`.

```
More = "Y"
```

This line should come before the `while` loop.

- ↗ **Add the new command before the loop to initialise the variable `More`**

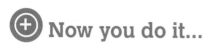 **Now you do it...**

Here is the complete program. The program includes the three new lines shown in this lesson.

```
## THE TOTALISER
## Demonstrate while loop
## Alison Page

print("========================")
print("Welcome to THE TOTALISER")
print("========================")

print("This program will add numbers together")

Total = 0
More  = "Y"

while More == "Y":
    number = input("Enter a number : ")
    number = int(number)
    Total  = Total + number
    More   = input("Enter another? (Y/N)")

print("the total is: ", Total)
```

1 Enter this code. Correct any errors. Save the program under a new name.

2 Run the program. Print out the code and the output to show your achievement.

🌐 If you have time...

↗ Add lines to the program to count how many times the loop repeats. You will need to make a new variable for this. Set the value to 0 before the loop begins. Add 1 to the variable with each iteration of the loop. Print out the value of this variable at the bottom of the program.

↗ Here is a bigger programming challenge. A programmer changed this program so that it did not use the variable More. Instead the loop would stop if the user entered the number 0. See if you can make this program.

📄 Test yourself...

1 What Python command is used to start a condition-controlled loop?

2 What are the four main relational operators in Python? Give the meaning of each one.

3 What is the data type of the variable More in this example?

4 A student changed one line of the program from this
       More = "Y"
   To this
       More = "N"
   What happened when the student ran the program? Test it and see whether you guessed correctly.

FACT

Strings

In Python, text strings can be enclosed in single or double quote marks. You can say 'Y' or "Y".

Key words

Condition-controlled loop: A condition-controlled loop is controlled by a logical test instead of a counter. It is also called a conditional loop.

Relational operator: A relational operator is a symbol that compares two values.

While loop: A while loop is the condition-controlled loop used in Python.

4.4 Make a List

Learning outcomes

In this chapter you have made a program that adds up a series of numbers to give the total. In this lesson you will change the program to save each number into a long list. At the end of the program you will be able to see the list of numbers as well as the total.

When you have completed this lesson you will be able to:

↗ store a sequence of values in a list

↗ find the total value of all the numbers in a list

↗ use Boolean operators.

⌘ Learn about...

You have learned that a variable is a named area of computer memory. You can store one value in a variable. For example, you might store a number or a string in a variable.

Often programmers want to store several values that all relate to the same subject. For example, a teacher might want to store the names of all her students. A bank might want to store the account balance for every customer.

The programmer could make many different variables. Each variable would have a different name and hold a different value. However, it is more convenient to make a **list variable**. One list variable can store lots of different values. The different values are called **items** in the list.

A list is shown in square brackets [ ]. The different items in the list are separated by commas. Here is an example: a web designer made a list of colours for a web site. The list looked like this:

```
Colourlist = ["Black", "Grey", "Red", "Violet"]
```

Append

You can **append** a value to a list. This adds the value to the end of the list. The designer appended "Indigo" to the list. The list looked like this:

```
Colourlist = ["Black", "Grey", "Red", "Violet", "Indigo"]
```

Colourlist now contains five items.

In this lesson you will make a number list by appending numbers one at a time.

Other names

In many programming languages, arrays are used instead of lists. Arrays and lists are similar but not identical structures. A list is made of items. An array is made of elements. Item and element mean more or less the same thing.

⏻ How to...

When the user runs the Totaliser program they enter a series of numbers. The program adds the numbers together. Now you will amend the program so that it also saves the numbers as a list.

To make this work you need to amend the Totaliser program. Here are the changes you will make.

1   *Before the loop:* Initialise the list.
2   *Inside the loop:* Append each number to the list.
3   *After the loop:* Print out the list.

Initialise the list

A list is enclosed in square brackets [ ]. At the start of the program you will initialise the list. At first the list is empty. The list is just square brackets.

```
Numberlist = []
```

In this example we have called the list `Numberlist`. You can call it any name.

↗   **Open the program you made**
↗   **Add a command at the top of the program code to initialise the list**

Append numbers to the list

Your program has a `while` loop. Remind yourself about the commands inside the loop. Look inside your own program. Can you find the command that does each of these tasks:

1   A command to input a value and store it as a variable called `number`?
2   A command to convert `number` to integer data type?
3   A command to add `number` to `Total`?

Now you will add a new command inside the loop. This command will append the variable number to the list `Numberlist`. Here is the command to do that.

```
Numberlist.append(number)
```

This command will be carried out every time the loop repeats.

↗   **Add the command to append the variable** `number` **to** `Numberlist`

Print the list

Finally, add a command at the end of the program to print out the list.
The command to do this is simple.

```
print(Numberlist)
```

This command will print out the whole list. You will see all the items that are inside square brackets.

↗   **Add the command to print** `Numberlist`

In *Matrix 3,* Chapter 4, Python, you will learn about more ways to work with lists. You will sort a list into order and look at the single items of the list.

 **Now you do it...**

Here is the complete program with all the commands you have learned.

1 Enter this code. Correct any errors. Save and run the program.

2 Print out the code and the output to show your achievement.

If you have time...

Here is an extension activity that is much longer than the previous ones you have done. Make sure you have completed the first part of this lesson before you try the extension activity. You may need a whole lesson to do the extension work.

A programming problem

A programmer made the Totaliser program, but she found there was a problem. Some users were typing the wrong thing. The prompt looks like this:

```
Do you want to add another number? (Y/N)
```

The conditional loop looks like this:

```
while More == "Y":
```

This logical test only works if the user enters an upper case Y. If the user types lower case y the loop will stop. Now you will fix this problem.

Boolean operators

You have learned about relational operators, such as < and >. Relational operators are used to make logical tests. A relational operator compares two values. The comparison can be 'true' or 'false'.

In this activity you will use a Boolean operator. **Boolean operators** join logical tests together to make a new composite test:

↗ The Boolean operator AND connects two tests together. The new composite test is 'true' if *both* tests are 'true'.

↗ The Boolean operator OR connects two tests together. The new composite test is 'true' if *at least one* test is 'true'.

↗ The Boolean operator NOT is added to a single test. The new composite test has the *opposite value* to the single test. If the single test is 'true', the composite test is 'false'. If the single test is 'false', the composite test is 'true'.

```
## THE TOTALISER
## Demonstrate while loop
## Alison Page

print("=======================")
print("Welcome to THE TOTALISER")
print("=======================")

print("This program will add numbers together")

Total = 0
More  = "Y"
Numberlist = []

while More == "Y":
    number = input("Enter a number : ")
    number = int(number)
    Numberlist.append(number)
    Total   = Total + number
    More    = input("Enter another? (Y/N)")

print("the list is ",   Numberlist)
print("the total is: ", Total)
```

In this activity you will use the OR operator.

Fixing the problem

In Python, Boolean operators are shown in lower case. The programmer decided to use the Boolean operator.

```
or
```

To join two tests together, she changed the first line of the `while` loop to this:

```
while More == "Y" or More == "y":
```

After this change the problem was fixed. The loop will work when the user types `Y` or when the user types `y`.

```
while More == "Y" or More == "y":
    number = input("Enter a number : ")
    number = int(number)
    Numberlist.append(number)
    Total   = Total + number
    More    = input("Enter another? (Y/N)")
```

✈ Make this change to your program. Run the program to see what happens.

 **Test yourself...**

1 Write the Python command to create an empty list called `Studentlist`.
2 Here is the Python code to append the name Thomas to `Studentlist`.

```
Studentlist.append("Thomas")
```

Write commands to append the names Sanjay and Mia to the list.
3 Write the Python command to print out the list called `Studentlist`.
4 Combine the answers to questions 1, 2 and 3 to make a complete Python program. Write the output you would see if you ran that program.

Key words

Append: To append is to add one item to the end of a list.

Boolean operator: A Boolean operator joins logical tests together to make a composite test.

Item: An item is a single value in a list.

List variable: A list is a single variable that can store a series of stored values.

Learning outcomes

You have created a program that stores a list of numbers and works out the total. In this lesson you will find out the largest number in the list.

When you have completed this lesson you will be able to:

↗ find the largest number in a list.

⌘ Learn about...

Programs often calculate an answer. You make a variable to store that answer. There are rules for naming a variable. Your variable name:

↗ must not have a space in it

↗ must start with a letter of the alphabet

↗ must include letters, numbers and underline only (no other symbols)

↗ must not use a word that already has a meaning in Python (such as input)

↗ should be a short, helpful name.

What is a helpful name? The name should remind you of what value is stored in that variable. That will make it easier for you to remember what the variable is for. Using helpful names will make it easier for you to read the program after you have written it.

Upper and lower case

Letters can be written in upper case (capital letters) or lower case (ordinary letters). Should you use upper or lower case in variable names? In most programming languages there is no firm rule, you can use either.

Some programmers like to use all lower case. In the Python language all commands are in lower case, so most Python programmers also stick to that rule for variable names. They might name a variable:

```
numberlist
```

Other programmers use upper case to show that a variable name is made of two words put together. For instance, they might name a variable:

```
NumberList
```

In this chapter some variables start with an upper-case letter to make them stand out in the text.

All these ways of making variable names will work. The only rule is that when you have decided on a variable name, you have to use that exact name throughout the program, otherwise the computer will not recognise the variable. Using the same pattern of upper and lower case in all your variables will make it easier to write code that works right first time.

If you ever work as a programmer, your team leader or workplace might have a rule about use of upper and lower case in variable names. Follow their rules.

Indentation

Indentation means that lines of code are set in from the left margin of the screen, so there is empty space at the start of the line. In some programming languages the programmer can add indentation if they want to. Indentation is used to make the program easier to read.

In Python, indentation is more important than that. Indentation shows you what lines belong inside a loop, or inside an `if` structure. Python adds the indentation automatically. Python starts adding indentation after a colon. The colon marks the start of a loop or an `if` structure.

You should turn the indentation off (by deleting it) if you want to stop putting commands inside the structure.

 **How to...**

Here is a simple program plan to find the largest value in a list.

1 *Before the loop:* Initialise a variable called `Largest`. Give it the value `0`.
2 *Inside the loop:* The user enters a number. Compare the number with `Largest`.
3 *If the number is bigger:* This number becomes `Largest`.

This plan will only work if the user enters a number bigger than zero. You will solve that problem in Lesson 4.6.

Before the loop

At the top of the program there are several lines of code that initialise variables. Each line shows the variable name and gives it a starting value.

```
Total = 0
More  = "Y"
Numberlist = []
```

Remember, Python chooses the data type based on the starting value. What is the data type for each of these variables?

↗ **Add a new line at the top of the program to initialise a variable called** `Largest` **with the value** `0`

What is the data type of this new variable?

Inside the loop

In *Matrix 1*, Chapter 4, Introducing Python, you learned to use the Python `if` command. An `if` command includes a logical test. In this program example you will add a logical test to see if the number entered by the user is the largest.

The variable `number` stores the value input by the user. Is the new number bigger than `Largest`? Here is the logical test:

```
if number > Largest:
```

The code after the logical test is only carried out if the result of the test is 'true'. This code is indented. Indentation is how Python shows that commands belong inside the `if` structure.

If the test result is 'true' then the value of the number is assigned to `Largest`.

```
if number > Largest:

    Largest = number
```

These two new lines go inside the `while` loop. This command will be carried out with every iteration of the loop.

```
while More == "Y" or More == "y":
    number = input("enter a number: ")
    number = int(number)
    Numberlist.append(number)
    Total   = Total + number

    if number > Largest:
        Largest = number

    More    = input("Add another? (Y/N): ")
```

Can you see that this program has a double indentation? The indented `if` goes inside the indented loop. A double indentation is called a **nested** structure. One set of indentation is nested inside another.

↗ **Add the `if` command inside the `while` loop to your code**

After the loop

At the bottom of the loop is a section where you print out the results.

```
print("\n")
print("RESULTS")
print("=======")
print("the list is:     ", Numberlist)
print("the total is:    ", Total)
print("the largest is: ", Largest)
```

↗ **At the bottom of the program, add a command to print out the largest number**

⊕ Now you do it...

1 Add code to calculate and display the largest number in the list.
2 Test the program using different input data.

🌐 If you have time...

Carry out a full range of tests on this program. In particular, try these tests.

↗ What happens if you enter a letter instead of a number?
↗ What happens if you press Enter without typing anything?
↗ What happens if all the numbers you enter are minus numbers?

Your tests should find problems with the program. In Lesson 4.6 we will fix those problems.

📄 Test yourself...

1 If a line of Python code ends with a colon (two dots), what does Python do to the next line of code?
2 A student started work in the school holidays doing programming for a small team. What rule should the student follow about using upper-case and lower-case letters in variable names?
3 Explain how you would choose a good name for a variable.
4 Explain what a nested code structure means.

Key words

Nested: If one indented structure is put inside another you get a double indentation. This is called a nested structure.

Learning outcomes

You have built a program that adds up a list of values. The program outputs a list of values and the largest value. In this lesson you will add input checks to make the program 'fool proof'.

When you have completed this lesson you will be able to:

↗ use validation to help prevent run-time errors.

 **Learn about...**

The 'If you have time...' activity in Lesson 4.5 asked you to test the program. If you did this, you will have found some problems with the program.

1 If you enter a letter instead of a number the program crashes.
2 If you press Enter without typing anything the program crashes.
3 If all the numbers you enter are minus numbers the largest is shown as 0.

Data type mismatch

If you type an input that is not a number (or if you don't enter any value) the program crashes. If you have not done it, try it now.

For example, we typed the letter 'x' instead of a number. The program **crashed**. We saw this error message.

```
=========================
Welcome to THE TOTALISER
=========================
This program will add numbers together
enter a number: x
Traceback (most recent call last):
  File "C:/Python34/Totaliser.py", line 16, in <module>
    number = int(number)
ValueError: invalid literal for int() with base 10: 'x'
```

The error message tells you that the program cannot carry out this command:

```
number = int(number)
```

It cannot convert the letter x into an integer. The data type does not match. This is an example of a run-time error. The syntax is OK, but when the user runs the program they can cause an error by entering the wrong type of data.

Validation

Of course, the user should not make errors like this. In real life, however, programmers have to plan for user errors. The programmer will add code to check input for errors.

Checking input is called **validation**. Validation checks that the input is valid before it is used in the program. There are many types of validation.

- ↗ Check that data is the right type.
- ↗ Check that a number is in the right range.
- ↗ Check that input is in line with any other program rules.

There is more than one way to add validation to a Python program. In this lesson you will do simple validation using an `if` command and a data type check.

 # How to...

Programming languages include commands called **functions**. A function takes in one value and produces a different value. There are functions to check the data type of a variable. We will use a function called:

```
isdigit()
```

This function can work on any string variable. The function checks to see if the value stored in the variable is made of digits. If the string variable is made of digits, it can be turned into an integer value. Just put the name of the variable before the function.

Here is the command to check the value stored in the variable `number`.

```
number.isdigit()
```

The result of this function is a true/false value. If the string IS made of digits, the result is 'true'. If the string is NOT made of digits, the result is 'false'.

`if... else` structure

You can use the `isdigit()` function as a logical test in an `if... else` structure.

1 `if` (the test result is 'true') convert the variable to the integer data type.

2 `else` (the test result is 'false') assign the value `0` to the variable.

Write the program code

Your program has this code in it. These lines are inside the `while` loop.

```
number = input("enter a number: ")
number = int(number)
```

We will put the `isdigit()` test in between these two lines. That means the conversion to integer will only be carried out if the value is made of digits.

```
number = input("enter a number: ")
if number.isdigit():
    number = int(number)
```

And finally, add an `else` section, so that if the value is NOT made of digits, the variable is given the value 0.

```python
number = input("enter a number: ")

if number.isdigit():

    number = int(number)

else:

    number = 0
```

Here is the complete program you made. Read through and make sure you understand all the code and what it does.

```python
print("=========================")
print("Welcome to THE TOTALISER")
print("=========================")
print("This program will add numbers together")

#initialise variables
Total = 0
Largest = 0
More  = "Y"
Numberlist = []

while More == "Y" or More == "y":
    number = input("enter a number: ")
    if number.isdigit():
        number = int(number)
    else:
        number = 0
    Numberlist.append(number)
    Total  = Total + number
    if number > Largest:
        Largest = number
    More   = input("Add another? (Y/N): ")


print("\n")
print("RESULTS")
print("=======")
print("the list is:     ", Numberlist)
print("the total is:    ", Total)
print("the largest is:  ", Largest)
```

⊕ Now you do it...

1   Write the new program code. The new code will add a validation check to the program.

2   Test the program and record the test results.

3   Print the program code and the output of the tests to show your achievement.

Here is an example of test results that you might see. The test data are 12, 77 and 3.

```
==========================
Welcome to THE TOTALISER
==========================
This program will add numbers together
enter a number: 12
Add another? (Y/N): y
enter a number: 77
Add another? (Y/N): y
enter a number: 3
Add another? (Y/N): n

RESULTS
=======
the total is     92
the largest is   77
the list is      [12, 77, 3]
```

Here is another example. The example shows what happens if someone enters invalid data. The user entered 100, then x, then a blank.

```
==========================
Welcome to THE TOTALISER
==========================
This program will add numbers together
enter a number: 100
Add another? (Y/N): y
enter a number: x
Add another? (Y/N): y
enter a number:
Add another? (Y/N): n

RESULTS
=======
the total is     100
the largest is   100
the list is      [100, 0, 0]
```

 # If you have time...

These challenging extension activities will test your programming ability. Only try them if you have plenty of time.

↗ Add an extra validation check to make sure the user does not input a value smaller than 0 (a minus number).

↗ If the user enters an invalid value, the number 0 is added to Numberlist. Change the program so that no number is added to Numberlist.

↗ Add validation to make sure that the user does not enter a value larger than 1000. Add commands to find the smallest number in the list.

Test yourself...

1 In this lesson you added an if… else structure to the program. What logical test did you use?

2 What happened if the result of the logical test was 'false'?

3 Explain why we add validation to a program.

4 A user tested the program. Instead of three numbers, she entered the values x, y and z. What was the output of this test?

Key words

Crash: A crash happens when a program stops working due to an error.

Function: A function is a command that takes in a value and gives out a different value.

Validation: Validation is checking input for errors before the input is used in the program.

Review what you have learned about Python

Overview

In this chapter you have learned how to:

- calculate values and assign them to variables
- select suitable data types, and convert variables to a new data type
- use condition-controlled and counter-controlled loops
- use arithmetic, relational and Boolean operators
- store a sequence of values in a list
- find the total value of all the numbers in a list
- find the largest number in a list
- use validation to help prevent run-time errors.

 Test questions

1 How does Python know what data type to use for a variable?

2 A counter-controlled loop began with this line

```
For i in range(30):
```
How often does this loop repeat?

3 A condition-controlled loop began with this line

```
while number < 5:
```
How can you stop this loop?

4 How does Python show which lines belong inside a loop structure?

5 Here is a command to make a list.

```
Materials = ["Diamond", "Graphite", "Steel"]
```
What is the command to add the word 'Tungsten' to this list? How many items are in the list now?

A dungeon exhibit in a museum was judged too upsetting for children under ten to see. Samira wrote a program to check the ages of people entering the museum. Here is the program. The program has several problems at the moment.

```
more = "Y"

while more == "Y":
    age = input("enter your age: ")
    age = int(age)
    if age < 10:
        print("you are too young to enter the dungeon exhibition")
    else:
        print("you may enter the dungeon exhibition")
```

6 She cannot stop the loop in the program. Say what line she needs to add to fix this problem.

7 The program asks users to input their age. If the user enters a letter instead of a number the program crashes. Explain how Samira can fix this problem.

8 What code could Samira add to store the ages of everyone coming into the museum and then print out the list at the end?

9 Samira wants to keep a count of the number of people who were too young to enter the dungeon room. What code can she add to the program and where will it go?

10 (*Extra challenge question—you will need a lot of time to complete this.*) Create a complete program for the museum, with all the problems fixed.

 ## Assessment activities

This program lets a bank customer withdraw money from his or her bank account. Withdraw means take money out of the bank account. Each time the person makes a withdrawal he or she has to enter the password.

```
AccountBalance = 100
Password = input("enter your password: ")

while Password == "1234":

    Withdraw = input("How much money do you want to withdraw? ")
    Withdraw = int(Withdraw)
    print("You have withdrawn: ", Withdraw)
    AccountBalance = AccountBalance - Withdraw
    print("Your new account balance is: ", AccountBalance)
    Password = input("Enter your password: ")
```

Starter activity

Make this program.

1 Change the password.

2 Change the amount the person has in his or her account to start with.

3 Run the program to make sure it works.

Intermediate activity

Change the program to add these features:

1 Add a validation check that the variable `Withdraw` holds a value made of digits before it is converted to integer data type.

2 Bank customers can only withdraw money if they have enough money in their account. Add a logical test that checks whether `Withdraw` is larger than `AccountBalance`. If the result of the check is 'true', show an error message. If the result of the check is 'false', bank customers can withdraw funds.

Extension activity

1 Add commands so that the value of each withdrawal is stored as a list. When the loop is finished, print out the list.

2 Amend the program so the user can also make deposits to the account. Deposit means to add money to the account. You will need to ask the user each time whether he or she wants to make a withdrawal or a deposit.

Information Technology

Across the web

Overview

In this chapter you will learn how computers communicate over the Internet. You will find out about the history of the World Wide Web. You will learn about searching the web, how the search results are ranked and how to narrow your search. You will also learn more about how to stay safe online. Think about the information you share. Can the information you share be removed or will that information stay online forever?

Learning outcomes

By the end of this chapter you will know how to:

- ↗ explain the difference between the Internet and the World Wide Web
- ↗ name pieces of network hardware and explain how they are used
- ↗ explain why the Internet needs protocols
- ↗ explain that data are sent in packets over the Internet
- ↗ understand that IP addresses help data get to the correct place
- ↗ describe how to do a simple search on the web
- ↗ narrow search results using advanced search tools
- ↗ explain how search engines work to rank search results
- ↗ clarify that images can stay on the web, even after they have been removed by the person who posted them
- ↗ stay safe on the web.

The Internet of Things

More and more household items have a computer. For example, if you have central heating, security lights or a refrigerator, these might all be controlled by computers. Household items can even be connected to the Internet to share data.

A house owner can control the temperature inside the house or watch video through a security camera, over the Internet. You can control household items when you are away from home. Smart fridges are connected to the Internet so you can check their contents while you are at the supermarket. In the future, your fridge might order your groceries for you online.

Which items in your life would you like to connect to the Internet? What would be the advantages and disadvantages of that item being connected? How would you use that item if it were connected to the Internet?

SMART HOME
Home Appliances with Internet of Things

FACT

The first webcam

We use webcams on our computers, phones and tablets to communicate. You can use Skype or FaceTime to see your friends while chatting. The first webcam was created in Cambridge. Its job was to watch a coffee pot, to see if the coffee was ready to drink.

xcoffee

This is the coffee pot as seen by the first webcam

Internet

WWW   Internet protocols

Packet-switched networks   Packets

Ranking   IP Address   Advanced Search

Creative Commons licence   Crawling

Indexing

Persistence of data

Learning outcomes

When you have completed this lesson you will be able to:

↗ understand the difference between the Internet and the World Wide Web

↗ explain why the Internet needs protocols.

 Learn about...

You can use the Internet as a tool to do many things. You can search the Internet to find answers to questions. You can watch videos to learn how to play a musical instrument, fix a car engine or crochet a quilt. You can find out how to unlock hidden features in a video game. You can send messages to your friends by text or live video. All of these examples can happen in seconds. This is all possible because of the Internet.

The Internet

In the 1950s computers were rare and only found in large organisations like universities and government departments. Computers were large. Computers usually filled whole rooms that were specially built to house them. No one owned a home computer and there was no Internet.

The organisations that did own computers wanted to use those computers to share information. In the 1960s computer scientists developed ways of connecting computers in different cities. The connections formed the first computer networks. A network that connects computers that are many miles apart is called a Wide Area Network (WAN). The first WAN, called ARPANET, was developed in the USA.

By the 1970s, people whose computers belonged to a particular WAN could share information with one another. Problems happened when they tried to share data between different WANs. Although the WANs all sent data in binary, they did it in different ways. Computers in different WANs could not understand each other.

By the 1980s, computer scientists had developed rules that let computers share data between WANs. These rules are called protocols. A protocol is a set of rules that are followed by everyone. All computers attached to the Internet must follow the same protocols when they organise and send data. This lets us view web pages, send emails and watch videos.

World Wide Web

Sir Tim Berners-Lee invented the World Wide Web (WWW) in 1990. Today the WWW is often shortened to 'the web'. Many people believe that the Internet and the WWW are the same. They are not.

- The **Internet** is a global network that can be accessed by any computer or network that follows agreed protocols. We can use a range of services that include the WWW, email and Internet telephony.
- The **WWW** is the part of the Internet that is made up of all the websites that exist across the world. We use a web browser to view the WWW.

The WWW is a method of creating pages on the Internet and linking them together with hyperlinks. You learned to create hyperlinks in *Matrix 1*, Chapter 6, Creative Communication. Remember, a hyperlink is a link on a web page that takes you to another page. Web pages today look much more sophisticated than the first web pages. But web pages still use the basic idea of hyperlinks that create a web of information.

The WWW is a way for all computer users to share information and view it using web browsers. You use web browsers every time you access the web. You might use a web browser such as Internet Explorer, Safari, Chrome or Firefox.

Two examples of websites are Facebook and the BBC website. A website will contain many web pages. On Facebook, those pages belong to users of the site. These users can post pictures and information about their interests. On the BBC website, the pages include news, information on sport, weather and TV programmes.

How big is the World Wide Web?

In 1990, the web contained only a few pages and was used mainly by computer scientists and researchers. The web has grown since then and continues to grow every day.

- The web is estimated to contain more than four billion pages (September 2016).
- More than three billion people use the web (2015).

 **How to...**

You can access the Internet using a web browser. The browser brings data from another computer on the Internet and displays the data as a web page.

- Open a browser on your computer.
- Browsers will vary slightly, but there is always an address bar towards the top left. In Chrome it looks like this:

Address bar

The WorldWideWeb (W3) is a wide-area hypermedia information retrieval initiative aiming t

↗ Every website has an address. The address is called a Unique Resource Locator (URL). CERN Laboratories in Switzerland have created a copy of the very first website. The CERN address is:

`http://info.cern.ch/hypertext/WWW/TheProject.html`

Typing this address into the address bar will display the page in your browser.

↗ This is what the web looked like in 1990.

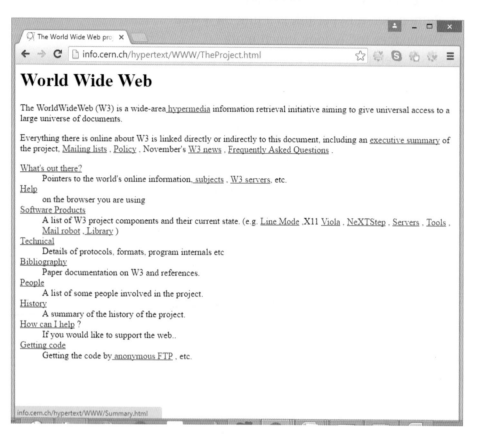

⊕ Now you do it...

You are going to look at a copy of the first web pages that were published in 1990. Then you will look at a modern web page and compare it with how a web page looked in 1990. You can work with a partner.

1 Open a web browser on your computer.

2 Type this URL into the address bar and press Enter.

`info.cern.ch/hypertext/WWW/TheProject.html`

3 A version of the first web pages will open in your browser window. Explore the site and make notes.

- What do hyperlinks look like? What happens if you click one?
- What does the site look like? Are there any pictures or animations? Does it use much colour?
- Can you find any games, social media, music or video?

- Return to the first page that says, 'World Wide Web' at the top. Click on the 'What's out there?' link, then click 'By subject'. How many resources were available in 1990? What resources were available for Maths?
- Would you use the World Wide Web of 1990?

4 Open a new browser tab.

5 Type this URL into the address bar and press Enter:

   `bbc.co.uk`

6 Explore the site and make notes using the same questions that you used for the 1990 World Wide Web.

7 How does today's web compare with that of 1990? Remember that the BBC site is only one of millions on today's World Wide Web.

 If you have time...

How do you use the World Wide Web? Every day you can use the web to communicate by sending emails, text messages or social media messages. You might watch television or a film online. You might listen to music or play an online game. Write a diary of how you use the web for a 24-hour period. How much time did you spend in each hour and what did you do?

Test yourself

1 What is a browser used for?

2 The Internet gives access to the WWW. Name another service the Internet provides.

3 Why does the Internet need protocols?

4 Describe how the World Wide Web has changed the lives of people you know.

Key words

Internet: The Internet is a global network that can be accessed by any computer or network that follows agreed protocols.

WWW: The World Wide Web is the part of the Internet that is made up of all the websites that exist across the world. The WWW is viewed by using a web browser.

Learning outcomes

When you have completed this lesson you will be able to:

↗ name pieces of network hardware and explain how they are used

↗ explain why the Internet needs protocols

↗ understand that IP addresses help data get to the correct place.

⌘ Learn about...

The Internet came about because people in universities and other organisations wanted to share data. At first, computer scientists were able to create a Wide Area Network (WAN) that could connect a small number of organisations together. However, they could not share information between WANs because each one had its own operating rules.

Two developments led to the Internet as we know it today. Those developments were:

↗ the development of common rules, also called protocols

↗ the development of hardware that lets computers connect to the Internet.

Network hardware

Computers are networked together using network hardware. Routers, modems, hubs, switches and bridges all connect computers to the Internet. Each piece of network hardware has its own job to do.

A router is an important piece of equipment for anyone who wants to connect to the Internet. The router's job is to connect two networks together. A router sends data from one network to another across the Internet. A router also receives the data that are returned. Your school will have a router. If you have an Internet connection at home you will have a router there too.

If you have a connection at home, it will probably use a wireless (Wifi) router. As the data comes into your home they are sent out as a wireless signal. You can pick up the signal anywhere in the house, or even outside in the garden.

Your home connection creates a mini Local Area Network (LAN). Several people can connect to the network and share files and other resources, such as a printer. Your school has a more sophisticated LAN. Using cables, the LAN connects together many computers and other devices, such as printers. Your school needs more equipment to connect all those devices to the school router.

A hub is a device that lets several computers share a single router. Your school may have several hubs. A hub has a single cable connecting it to the router. A hub also has a cable that connects it to each computer in its network. When a hub receives a message from the router, it sends the message to all the computers in its network. The message is processed only by the computer that the message was addressed to. A switch does the same job as a hub, only a switch is smarter.

A switch knows the name of each device it is connected to. A switch only sends data where those data are meant to go. If data contain a document to be printed, then a switch sends the document directly to the printer. The switch does not send that document to all devices on the network.

A Local Area Network switch

If your school has a wireless network, it will use a more sophisticated version of a home wireless router. A wireless router is connected to the main router. The wireless router acts as a switch and is connected by cable to wireless access points (WAPs) around the school. WAPs are usually installed in the ceiling. There should be enough WAPs to make sure a good wireless signal is available everywhere in the building.

There is other equipment that we can use in particular situations. A bridge is another kind of switch, but a bridge joins Local Area Networks together. We use a modem if the Internet is carried to a location along a phone line. Using a modem is much more likely in the home than in a school or office. Data sent over a phone line have to be converted into digital data before they can be sent over a LAN. The modem converts between the phone signal and digital data.

Connecting to the Wifi

Internet protocols

Internet protocols are the rules computers use to make sure data can be sent and understood across the Internet. There are different protocols for sending and receiving data. Some of the more important Internet protocols are:

- ↗ TCP/IP Internet protocols control how data are sent from one network to another. A message is split into small packets of data and put back together by the computer that receives them.
- ↗ Hyper Text Transfer Protocol (HTTP) controls how web pages are built and sent over the Internet so they can be viewed in a browser. HTTP appears at the start of every web address in your browser address bar.
- ↗ Post Office Protocol (POP3), Simple Mail Transfer Protocol (SMTP) and Internet Message Access Protocol (IMAP) all set the rules for different ways of sending emails.

There are many other Internet protocols. For example, FTP (File Transfer Protocol) is used to send files. Each Internet protocol sets out guidelines or rules. The Internet and WWW would not be possible without these protocols.

Internet Protocol Address (IP address)

There are over four billion web pages on the WWW. How do we find a web page when we want to read it? Every web page is stored on a computer somewhere in the world. That computer is called a web server. A web server serves web pages to the Internet.

In the same way that your house has an address, your computer has an address too. The postal service can deliver a letter to your house because your address is unique. It is the same with the Internet. Every computer on the Internet has its own unique address. The way that computers are addressed is set by rules in the Internet Protocol. The address of the computer is called the Internet Protocol Address **(IP address)**. That address might look like this: 198.51.100.3

 How to...

You can find your computer's IP address by using a web browser and a website such as: `whatsmyip.org`

Type the website name into the address bar at the top of your web browser. A new web page will open and it will show the IP address at the top.

 Now you do it...

How do you connect to the Internet? You might use a phone, tablet, laptop or PC. Each of these devices has an IP address.

Use the website `whatsmyip.org` to find the IP address for the device you are currently using. Then try different devices. For example, what is the IP address of your mobile phone or laptop?

Convert the decimal numbers into binary numbers for the IP address you have found. Ask a partner to check to see if they agree with your answer.

If you have time...

Each computer has an IP address. Websites are stored on computers. When you type the address of a website into your web browser, the browser looks up the IP address for the computer on which the site is stored. Web addresses are easier to type as words than numbers, but we can type the IP address of the website instead. For example, the `apple.com` website is held on a computer with the IP address: 17.178.96.59

Try typing this IP address into the address box of your web browser. Does it take you to the Apple website?

 # Test yourself...

1 What do the letters IP stand for?
2 Give an example of a computer protocol. What is the protocol for?
3 Why do computers need an IP address?
4 Why do we type words into the address bar rather than the IP address numbers?

Key words

Internet protocols: Internet protocols are sets of rules that are followed by all computers. Computers can view web pages, send emails and show videos, because they organise data using protocols.

IP address: An IP address is the electronic address of the computer. IP stands for Internet Protocol. This means that every computer connected to the Internet is given an address, following the set of instructions for the Internet Protocol. The address might look like this 198.51.100.3

Learning outcomes

When you have completed this lesson you will be able to:

↗ explain that data are sent in packets over the Internet

↗ understand that IP addresses help data get to the correct place.

⌘ Learn about...

Imagine you need to post a book to a friend, but you can only send small envelopes in the mail. The envelopes are too small to contain the whole book. What do you do? You could divide your book into smaller sections and post each one in a numbered envelope. Your friend could then put the book back together when all of the envelopes have arrived. If you keep a copy of your book for a while, your friend could ask you to re-send any parts of the book that did not arrive.

That is how messages are sent across the Internet. This is described in a protocol called TCP/IP. TCP stands for Transmission Control Protocol. TCP says how the book is divided and how it is put back together again. IP stands for Internet Protocol and says how the envelope is addressed to reach its destination. The two protocols work together to send messages so we call them as TCP/IP.

You can use TCP/IP to send and receive data between computers on the Internet. The TCP protocol tells the computer to break the data into small groups called **packets**. Packets are like the envelopes you used to send the book. A packet, like the envelope, contains the data that you are sending. The IP address gives the packet's destination.

Every web page and every email is transmitted across the Internet as a series of packets. The packets are put back together by the receiving computer. The packets must be put back together in the correct order or they would not make sense.

The TCP/IP protocol tells the computers how to break the data into packets and also how to put them together again. This makes using packets very reliable. If one computer or part of the network is broken, then the packets can find another route to their destination. If the computer receiving a message finds a packet is missing, it can request that only the missing packet be re-sent from the original computer. A single packet can be re-sent instead of re-sending all of the data.

⏻ How to...

A computer converts an email into binary data to store and process it. Before it sends the data, the computer breaks the binary data up into packets of a fixed size. A packet sent over the Internet is usually from 20 bytes up to 1500 bytes in size.

Each packet contains a small part of the email. The packet also contains vital information that makes sure that the email arrives safely and complete at its destination.

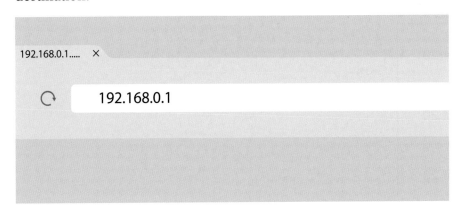

Imagine sending an email to a friend. The data in the email need to be broken into packets. Each packet includes the:

- ⬈ IP address of the sender
- ⬈ IP address of the receiving person's computer
- ⬈ total number of packets in the email
- ⬈ number of that individual packet
- ⬈ length of the packet
- ⬈ main body text of the email
- ⬈ the name of the protocol that has been used—TCP/IP.

Each packet is sent separately to its destination. The packets might travel by different routes. If there is a problem with one part of the network, the packets will follow another route. The packets taking different routes are like a fleet of mail vans avoiding road traffic.

The data in the packet tells the receiving computer the total number of packets to expect. The receiving computer checks to make sure the packets have all arrived. If any packets are missing, the receiving computer asks the sending computer to re-send them. When all the packets have arrived the receiving computer is able put the original email message back together.

The Internet is an example of a **packet-switched network**. Messages are divided into packets, which reach their destinations through a series of switches or routers. It is not just emails that are sent in this way. All data sent across the Internet are sent in packets of binary code. Everything from a music track you download to a question you send to a search engine, is sent as packets of binary data.

Now you do it...

Search online to find a picture of a famous person.

1   Print out the picture you have found and draw a grid over the whole picture. The grid should have four columns and five rows.

2   Number each grid rectangle, starting with 1 in the top left corner.

3   Write '1 of 20', then in the next column '2 of 20', and the next column '3 of 20', and so on until you fill the grid.

1 of 20	2 of 20	3 of 20	4 of 20
5 of 20	6 of 20	7 of 20	8 of 20
9 of 20	10 of 20	11 of 20	12 of 20
13 of 20	14 of 20	15 of 20	16 of 20
17 of 20	18 of 20	19 of 20	20 of 20

4   Draw the same grid and write the same numbers on another blank piece of paper.

5   Cut up the picture of the famous person, cutting along the grid lines. You should have 20 grid rectangles with a picture in the background. Do not cut the blank grid paper.

6   Work as a whole class on this part. Place the blank grid at one end of the room. Ask everyone to find a space around the room and stand still. One person should stand next to the blank grid.

7   Take the cut up pieces to the opposite end of the room to the blank grid and stand still.

8   Pass random grid pieces to the people nearest you. The people nearest you then pass random pieces on to the next person. The pieces should be moving around the room towards the blank grid.

9   The person next to the blank grid places the pieces of the picture on top of the numbered rectangles, as each one arrives.

10 When all the pieces have arrived, you can stop.

The pieces of the picture have followed different routes across the network. Sometimes the pieces followed the same route. All of the pieces arrived in the end and the picture was reconstructed following the protocol. The protocol was the way the grid was numbered. You knew all the pieces had arrived because the total number of pieces was written on each one, for example, 5 of 20.

 ## If you have time...

You can send two pictures to two addresses, A and B.

1   With the current picture you have from the 'Now you do it...' activity, label each grid rectangle 'A' under the existing numbers.

2   Find a second picture and print it out. Cut it up and number the rectangles as you did with the first picture.

3   Label each grid rectangle 'B' under the numbers. The existing blank grid will be destination 'A'.

4   Create a second blank grid. This will be destination 'B'.

5   Jumble up all of the rectangles for the two pictures.

6   Repeat the 'Now you do it...' activity, this time passing all rectangles labelled 'A' to destination A, and all rectangles labelled 'B' to destination B.

The pieces of the picture have followed different routes across the network. All of the pieces arrived and the picture was reconstructed following a protocol. The protocol is the way the grid was numbered. You knew all the pieces had arrived, because the total number of pieces was written on each one, for example, 5 of 20.

 ## Test yourself...

1   Why is each packet that makes up an email numbered?

2   What information is included with a packet to help it get to the correct destination?

3   How does a computer know it has received all of the packets?

4   What happens if one of the packets meets a blockage in the network?

FACT

Email and text messages

An email is just a piece of text sent to a recipient. Today, we can add attachments that make messages longer. Even with attachments, however, email messages are still text messages. Attached binary files, such as images, are converted into a text-based code, where letters represent binary numbers. When the attachment is received, it is converted from text back into binary to re-create the original file.

Key words

Packets: Packets are small groups of binary data that computers transfer using the Internet. Every web page that you receive comes as a series of packets. Every email you send is divided into a series of packets and sent across the Internet.

Packet-switched network: Packet-switched networks move data around in packets. Packet-switched networks use switches to route the packets to their destinations.

Learning outcomes

When you have completed this lesson you will be able to:

↗ describe how to do a simple search on the web

↗ explain how search engines work to rank search results.

⌘ Learn about...

How do you find the answer to a question? Where do you look? You might say, "I will just Google it" meaning you are going to search the web using the search engine created by Google. A search engine is a website that specialises in searching the World Wide Web. Google is an example of a popular search engine. There are many search engines. Bing, Yahoo and DuckDuckGo are other examples of search engines.

Think carefully about the words you use to search

When searching the web, you need to choose the words you enter into the search box carefully. The search engine will use the words you have chosen to find relevant web pages. The search engine will rank the results based on a complicated algorithm.

When you search for information with a search engine you need to read and evaluate the search results to decide which will be the most useful and reliable. The search engine tries to help you by ranking the results. **Ranking** is how the search engine organises the result of a search. The results are ranked in order of the most relevant information for that search.

Punctuation and search operators

If you find a search returns too many results, you can narrow your search to get closer to the results you want. You can use punctuation to help your search.

You can use quotation marks to make sure your search only returns the pages that exactly match the text between the quotes. For example, if you search using "Steve Jobs" with quotation marks, then only results containing the two words together will be found.

You can also narrow your search by using symbols. For example, you can use a minus symbol before the word or words you want to search on. If you use a minus symbol, your search results will produce web pages that do *not* contain those search word(s).

You can also use search operators to narrow a search. One example of a search operator is 'site:'.

You can add 'site:' to your search words to search within a particular website. For example, you might be learning about the Egyptian King Tutankhamun and only want to search the BBC website.

You could use this search string:

```
Tutankhamun site:bbc.co.uk
```

If you want to look up the meaning of a particular word, or see if the word has different spellings, use 'define:' followed by the word.

Try using this search term in Google:

```
define:Tutankhamun
```

The search results show that Tutankhamun was a pharaoh in Egypt who lived sometime around 1400 BC. If you scroll down your search results, you will see that some websites spell the name differently: Tutankhamen.

Google has information on how to make your search efficient and narrow your results. You can do a Google search on 'Search operators' to find out more.

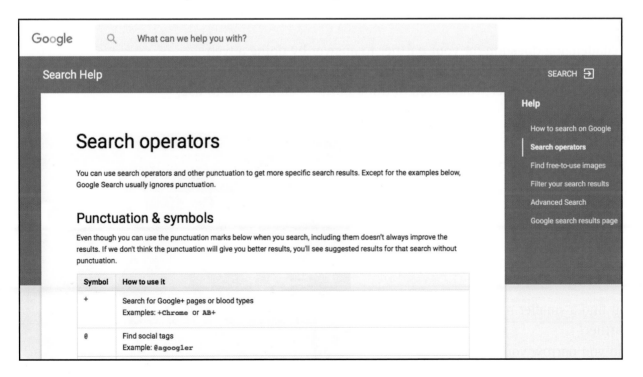

 **How to...**

Look at the website created by Google, which explains how a Google search works.

`https://www.google.co.uk/insidesearch/howsearchworks/thestory/`

1 The first step in a search is called **crawling**. Search engines use 'bots'. Bot is short for 'software robot'. A bot works automatically to do the same job as a human, but much faster. Search engine bots 'crawl' over the web following the hyperlinks between web pages. They gather information about the pages they visit.

2 In the second step, the information gathered is used to create an index of the web. This process is called **indexing**. This is like the index of a book but much bigger. For example, Google's index contains over 100 million gigabytes of data. Indexing happens all the time, not just when you make a search request.

3 The third step is to work through the index to find pages that match your search request. The search engine uses complex algorithms to find the web pages that match your request. When you do a web search, the algorithms try to sort the results, placing the most useful results at the top of the list. Different search engines use different algorithms so the search results can be different. Search engines tend to keep their algorithms secret, but there are some common approaches. For example, if a website has links from many other sites, it will tend to be given more importance in the ranking.

4 The fourth step is to remove spam. Spam is unwanted information. Spam can be removed by algorithms but also by people working for the search engine company.

Now you do it...

Think of a challenging question for your partner to answer by doing a web search. For example, you might ask your partner, "Which movie made the most money last year?" Your partner would need to think of the search words to use, such as:

`most money movie`

Your partner could then narrow the search by:

- looking within a particular website
- using quotation marks to search for exact words or phrases.

You should also look for results for the same question.

- Can you find a smaller number of results than your partner?
- How did you narrow your search?

If you have time...

A trend is when many people search for a similar word or topic. A search can be trending if there is a breaking news story. Google Trends shows searches by category and by location. Open the website at www.google.com/trends/ and see the top trends for the USA. Change the location selector on the page to where you live.

↗ What are the top stories today?

↗ Look at a national news website.

↗ Are the top stories on the news website the same as the top trends on Google?

 # Test yourself...

1 Name three web browsers.

2 Describe how you would search for information on the President of the USA.

3 How can a search be narrowed to only search a particular website?

4 Why would you use quotation marks in a web search?

FACT

Use your voice

The Google search app has an integrated voice search. If your device has the Google search app and a microphone, open the app and say, "OK, Google." You can then say the words for your search. Google will automatically search those words and display the results.

Key words

Crawling: Crawling is the first step a search engine takes when gathering information about web pages. A piece of software called a bot visits each web page and follows the links to other pages.

Indexing: Indexing is the second step a search engine takes when gathering information about web pages. All of the information gathered by the bots is put together in an index. The information can then be organised and ranked.

Ranking: Ranking is a way to organise the information returned from web searches. When you search for information using a search engine, the results are ranked in order of the most relevant information for that search.

Learning outcomes

When you have completed this lesson you will be able to:

↗ describe how to do a simple search on the web

↗ narrow search results using advanced search tools.

⌘ Learn about...

How can you make your searches more accurate? You can think carefully about the words you enter into the search box. You can add extra instructions to the search. You can also use advanced search features provided by search engines.

Many search engines have an **advanced search** feature. Advanced search features help to narrow the search and make the search more effective. You will explore some of the ways you can use advanced features in this lesson.

A search engine looks for images as well as web pages on the World Wide Web. The advanced search features can, for example, find images that are available under a **Creative Commons licence**. A Creative Commons licence is a way for creators to give permission to others to use images, text, videos and audio. A Creative Commons licence makes it clear whether you can use an image and what for.

If you find a photo on the Internet and want to use it for something, make sure you have permission. A Creative Commons licence makes it easy to see if you have permission. If you cannot find a Creative Commons licence, make sure you contact the owner of the image for permission to use it.

⏻ How to...

You carry out a search by using key words. For example, to find out about the British astronaut, Tim Peake, you can enter his first name and surname. A search using Tim Peake's first name and surname could return about 550,000 results. How can you make the number of results smaller?

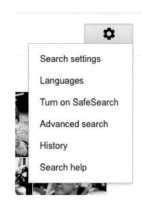

If you are using Google in a web browser, select the cog icon on the right side of the screen. You will see a drop-down list. Choose the Advanced search option to display the Advanced Search page.

The Advanced Search page gives options to search for exact words. You can also remove a particular word or search within a range of numbers.

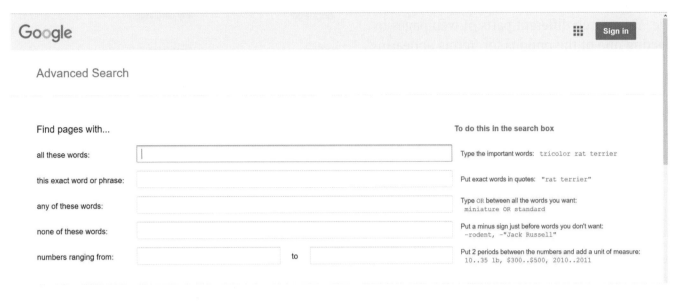

You can then narrow the search even further. You can search for your exact words in a particular language. The search will return all pages that contain the search words in a particular language. For example, the language could be changed to English to return only pages written in English. The region option can return pages from a certain part of the world.

The search option 'last update' is important. Last update helps you search for web pages that have been updated within a certain time period. For example, your search could look for pages that have been updated:

↗ anytime
↗ in the past 24 hours
↗ in the past week
↗ in the past month
↗ in the past year.

If you are looking for pictures of your favourite band on their latest tour, you can search for images that have been posted in the past week or within the past 24 hours.

If you really want to narrow your search, you can search the different parts of web pages, including the title, the web address and the links on the page. You search different parts of web pages by selecting one of the options for 'terms appearing'.

The 'usage rights' option can help when you are searching for images. Different images have different permissions to reuse them. For example, you may want to find an image of Tim Peake that you can use in your work. The images are owned by the people who made them. Some photographers might want to sell their images. Others may be happy to allow anyone to use their image.

Google image searches have their own Advanced Search page. After your initial search, click Images at the top of the search results page to show images instead of web pages. Select the cog icon at the top right of the page as before and select Advanced Search. The Advanced Search page for images will be shown.

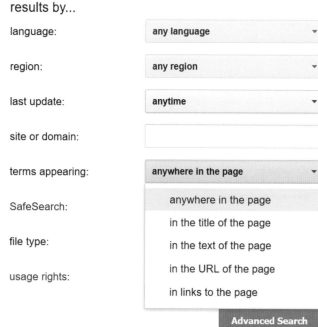

The number of search results should become smaller each time you add an Advanced Search feature. Advanced Search features make the search more efficient and help you towards the most relevant results for your search.

Then narrow your results by...

image size:	any size	Find images in any size you need.
aspect ratio:	any aspect ratio	Specify the shape of images.
colours in the image:	● any colour ○ full colour ○ black & white ○ transparent ○ this colou	Find images in your preferred colours.
type of image:	any type	Limit the kind of images that you find.
region:	any region	Find images published in a particular region.
site or domain:		Search one site (like `sfmoma.org`) or limit your results to a domain like `.edu`, `.org` or `.gov`
SafeSearch:	Show most relevant results	Tell SafeSearch whether to filter sexually explicit content.
file type:	any format	Find images in the format that you prefer.
usage rights:	not filtered by licence	Find images that you are free to use.

not filtered by licence

free to use or share

free to use or share, even commercially

free to use share or modify

free to use, share or modify, even commercially

You can also...

Find pages that are similar to or link to a URL

Now you do it...

The 'a Google a day' website sets a challenge for people to solve. Look at the website:

`agoogleaday.com`

Each day a new challenge appears. The website states, "There's no right way to solve it, but there's only one right answer."

1   Work with a partner to see who can find the answers the fastest.

2   Choose the Start Playing button for the first question.

3   Can you use your Advanced Search techniques to narrow your search and find the answer?

 If you have time...

You can use the SafeSearch option on Google's Advanced Search page. The SafeSearch option removes websites that are unsuitable for children from the search results.

1   Try searching for information on your favourite team or activity.

2   Record the number of results you find.

3   Use the Settings cog to select Turn on SafeSearch.

4   Now repeat your search and see if the number of results is different.

The Safe Search website has the safety features already switched on:

`http://primaryschoolict.com`

Try searching for information about a celebrity using both the Google front page with the SafeSearch turned on and the Safe Search website (`primaryschoolict.com`). Which one is easier to use?

Test yourself...

1   How do you search for key words used in the last 24 hours?

2   What is a safe search?

3   When should you use the Advanced Search features?

4   Who is able to say how an image or piece of text can be used?

Key words

Advanced Search: Advanced Search is a feature on a search engine that helps to narrow the search. An Advanced Search can help find results with specific key words or find web pages that have been updated recently.

Creative Commons licence: A Creative Commons licence is a way for creators to give permission to others to use text, images, videos and audio. If someone else uses your photo, you can also say that they have to share it on the same terms that you did. This is called a Share Alike license.

FACT

Google searches

In 2016, 40,000 searches were being sent to Google every second. That adds up to 3.5 billion searches a day. When Google was launched in 1998, the number of searches a day was only 10,000.

According to Google, a search request makes an average round trip of 1500 miles before the result gets back to you.

5.6 Following your route online

Learning outcomes

When you have completed this lesson you will be able to:

↗ understand that images can stay on the web, even after they have been removed by the person who posted them

↗ stay safe on the web.

⌘ Learn about...

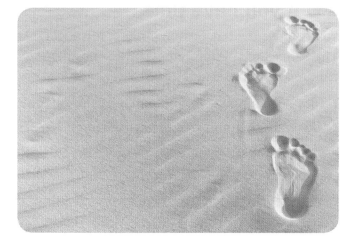

Every time you go online you leave a trail. Imagine walking down a sandy beach. Your footprints show the route you have taken through the sand. Each search engine or web browser has a History section that shows the route you have taken online. Your computer has a unique IP address. The company that provides your connection to the Internet records your IP address. The company can also record the IP addresses of the sites you visit. This record shows where you have been online.

Think about what you talk about with your friends. You might mention people, places, hobbies, bands and sports. You might talk about things you like and dislike. All of these topics create a picture of who you are and what you are interested in. You probably search the web looking for similar things. You might look for the details of a band or use social media to share an image with a friend. All of these interactions leave a trail about you, showing where you have been online.

Persistence of data on the web

In the past cameras might only be used at special occasions, such as a birthday party or a wedding. We now have access to cameras on our phones every day. It is easy to take an image and capture a happy moment or a video of our friends. It is easy to share these images and videos online so that your friends can see them too. One of the benefits of technology is that it enables sharing and lets us keep in touch with our friends.

You need be careful what information you share about yourself online. You need to think about who can see the images and videos that you share. Is it only you and your friends who can see your information, or can the friends of your friends see it? Can the whole world see your information? Many social networking tools let you post images, videos and text online. You need to check the settings to make sure only the people you want to see your information can see it.

You might think you are taking an image off the web when you delete it from your social media website or app. However, once you have shared your information, it can sometimes still be found. For example, a person may have taken a copy of your image and stored it on their phone or computer.

Some websites store old versions of different sites for historical records. For example, the Wayback Machine is an online library that stores old versions of websites even after the websites have been deleted. You can view copies of these older websites at:

http://archive.org/web/

Persistence of data describes when the data are still available, even when they may not be needed or wanted anymore. With an image, the person who owns the image may have removed it but the data may still be available on the web.

 How to...

You might post an image online of yourself and your friends. Different social media tools, for example, Facebook, encourage you to post an image and comment on other peoples' images. You need to be 13 or older to have a Facebook account. This is the same for many other social media tools.

The number of social media sites is constantly growing. Each type of social media site can offer a different way of interacting with another person or group of people. People may choose a social media website because of its features or because their friends and family are already using it.

Some people use Snapchat, a social media tool, to share photos and videos. Snapchat claims that the photos and videos can only be viewed by the recipient for one to ten seconds before the images disappear forever. However, the person who receives the images could take a screenshot. So, the photo does not disappear and someone could post it again.

There are many benefits to communicating online with friends and family. However, you need to carefully consider what you post online because that data can be persistent.

You need to be careful what you share on all social media sites. Always tell a trusted adult (for example, a teacher or parent) if something online upsets you.

Staying safe with social media

There are many sites on the Internet that offer advice on staying safe online. Your teacher may provide links to sites that are useful and relevant for you. To stay safe online, you should follow these guidelines:

1   Don't post any personal information online—keep your address and phone number private.
2   Never give out your password.
3   Think carefully before you post an opinion or picture online. What you post could be difficult to remove. How will your comments or pictures make you look to other people now and in the future?

4   Only accept friend requests from people you know.

5   Do not meet up with people you meet online. If people suggest you do meet, speak to a parent or responsible adult. Not everyone online is who they say they are.

6   If you see something online that makes you feel uncomfortable, unsafe or worried, tell an adult.

7   If you feel you are being bullied online, speak to an adult.

And finally, behave responsibly yourself. Respect other people's views, even if you don't agree with them.

⊕ Now you do it...

What does the word 'persistent' mean? You can find out using a search engine. You could use the search terms, 'define:persistent'.

Design a presentation titled 'Staying safe online'. Give the presentation to all of the students in your year group. Many students will be thinking about using social media sites, such as Facebook. Your presentation should give advice on how your fellow students can stay safe online. Include something that encourages students to think about the persistence of the information that they post online. How might the persistence of data affect students in the future?

⊕ If you have time...

A selfie is a photo of a person that they have taken themselves. People often take selfies:

↗   with celebrities

↗   in famous places

↗   with their friends

↗   on their own.

Do you think people should post selfies online? Are they giving away too much information? What should a person do if they share a photo and then change their minds and want to remove it?

 Test yourself...

1   Why should you care about data persistence?

2   Who should you tell, if you find something upsetting online?

3   Should you share your password with anyone you do not know?

4   Should everyone have a social media account?

FACT

Fake news sites

There are websites that provide fake news stories. These websites are read by people who sometimes share the fake stories on social media sites. Sharing these stories on social media can cause the fake stories to circulate widely. You can check if the story is true. Use a search engine to see if you can find the story on a reputable website.

Key words

Persistence of data: Persistence of data describes when the data are still available, even when they may not be needed or wanted anymore. This can be a problem if you put have an image online on social media and then remove it afterwards. The image may still be available if someone has copied it or if an archive of the website has been kept.

Review what you have learned about information technology

Overview

In this chapter we have learned about the Internet, the World Wide Web and staying safe online.

You have learned how to:

↗ explain the difference between the Internet and the World Wide Web

↗ name pieces of network hardware and explain how they are used

↗ explain why the Internet needs protocols

↗ explain that data are sent in packets over the Internet

↗ understand that IP addresses help data get to the correct place

↗ describe how to do a simple search on the web

↗ narrow search results using advanced search tools

↗ explain how search engines work to rank search results

↗ clarify that images can stay on the web, even after they have been removed by the person who posted them

↗ stay safe on the web.

Test questions

1   What is the Internet?

2   What is the World Wide Web?

3   Name three web browsers.

4   Why do computers need an IP address?

5   What is a network packet?

6   Why do packets travel to their destination by different paths?

7   What is an Advanced Search?

8   What is meant by persistence of data?

9   What action would you take if you were bullied online?

10 Describe how your life would change if the World Wide Web was no longer available.

Assessment activities

You can search for information using the World Wide Web. The websites are held on computers across the world. The computers are joined together as a huge network called the Internet. You are going to learn about a Space topic using this great resource.

Starter activity

Open a web browser and search for "Who was the first man to walk on the moon?"

- ↗ How could you simplify your search? Instead of writing the whole sentence, which words could you leave out?
- ↗ What was the name of the space mission for the first moon landing?
- ↗ Search to find out the names of the two other people who were on the moon landing mission.

Intermediate activity

Your search can be narrowed by using some search tips. Narrow your search to find:

- ↗ a word in the title of a website
- ↗ a definition of a word
- ↗ a missing or joining word
- ↗ the results minus a particular word
- ↗ the exact word or phrase
- ↗ a particular file type.

Extension activity

Look at the Advanced Search features for your search for the first person on the moon. Narrow your search to find results:

- ↗ updated in the past month
- ↗ only in English
- ↗ in the range of years from 1968 to 1970
- ↗ filtered using a Safe Search
- ↗ that can be shared under the non-commercial Creative Commons licence.

Create a news report for the moon landing. Research information and add images that can be used under the Creative Commons licence.

6 Creative Communication

Developing a website

Overview

In this chapter you will learn some advanced features of HTML (Hypertext Markup Language) and CSS (Cascading Style Sheets). You will use these features to create a website. Your website will have more than one web page. You will learn how to create a simple navigation bar using a text editor. You will also conduct research and analyse data. This information will then be added to your website.

Learning outcomes

By the end of this chapter you will know how to:

- ↗ create a basic web page
- ↗ plan and create the basic structure of a web page
- ↗ understand the difference between HTML and CSS
- ↗ identify reliable websites
- ↗ add a simple left-hand menu to a web page
- ↗ understand margins, content, padding and borders
- ↗ understand and edit divisions, elements and attributes
- ↗ insert local and external hyperlinks
- ↗ insert a hyperlink to an email
- ↗ use text and images as a hyperlink
- ↗ use data to create a graph
- ↗ save a graph as a web page
- ↗ analyse data and make a judgement.

Talk about...

Work in a group to list all the different sources of information available to you. Discuss the advantages and disadvantages of each source and share your ideas with the class.

F|A|C|T

The Father of Email

Programmer Ray Tomlinson (1941–2016) is widely known as the 'father of email'. He decided on the @ sign used in email addresses today. Ray Tomlinson changed computing by improving the way we communicate with each other, and made it possible for us to keep in touch from wherever we are in the world.

CSS

Site map   Padding

HTML   **Style sheet**   Content

Source code   Bias

Axes

External link   **Wireframe**

Trend

Key   Border   Margin

Hyperlink   GUI

Local link

Learning outcomes

When you have completed this lesson you will be able to:

↗ use HTML to edit or create basic web pages

↗ create the basic structure of a web page.

⌘ Learn about...

You can use HyperText Markup Language (**HTML**) to build and create web pages. HTML uses elements and tags to create a web page.

Tags mark the beginning and the end of an element. An element includes everything from the start to the end of a tag.

For example, this line is a paragraph element:

< p > I am learning to code < /p >

The tags that start and end the element are:

< p > and < /p >

You can also use elements to format the text on your web page.

You can use more than one element on a simple piece of text. Elements and tags can be inserted inside each other. This is called nesting. When nesting, remember to close the tags in reverse order. For example:

< b > < u > < i > Computing < /i > < /u > < /b >

You can link your web page to other web pages or documents using a hyperlink. A hyperlink is an image, graphic or piece of text that links your web page to another page or document. You can move from one web page to another by clicking the hyperlink.

You can see the code used to create a web page by viewing the **source code** of that page. The source code shows the commands or instructions used to create a web page. The code you see will depend on the language used to create the web page. The way you access the source code will depend on your web browser.

Software

All you need to write HTML is a text editor such as Notepad. There are many software tools available to help you create professional web pages, even if you cannot write in HTML.

Microsoft Expression Web 4 and Adobe Dreamweaver are professional tools for designing, developing, and publishing websites. You can create a web page using Adobe Dreamweaver or Microsoft Expression Web 4 using the graphical user interface (**GUI**) or by writing code. A GUI (sometimes pronounced 'gooey') interacts with the computer using icons and menus rather than text. Using a product with a GUI means that you do not have to write code to create your web page. You can use icons, just like you do when you create a document in Microsoft Word. Web design software that works using a GUI is known as WYSIWYG software (sometimes pronounced 'wizzywig'). WYSIWYG stands for, "What you see is what you get". The term WYSIWYG describes software that allows you to edit text and graphics in a form which looks like the finished product. You do not have to write code. There are many other web design products available.

In this lesson, we will concentrate on Microsoft Expression Web 4. Microsoft Expression Web 4 is available free to download.

 # How to...

You need to know how to use simple tags when you create a web page. Here is a review of what you learned about using tags in *Matrix 1*, Chapter 6, Creative Communication.

Inserting elements and tags

Doctype declaration `<!DOCTYPE html>`: this tells the browser what language it is reading by defining the document type. **The Doctype declaration must be the first tag on your page. This tag does not need to be closed.**

HTML tags `<html>` `</html>`: this identifies the beginning and the end of the page.

Head tags `<head>` `</head>`: this gives information about the page. **The head tag must only be used once. It should be used after the opening HTML tag.**

Title tag `<title>` `</title>`: identifies what the page is called. You can see the title in the browser's title bar or tab. The title tag should go between the Head tags.

Body tags `<body>` `</body>`: the text or images between these tags will be visible on your web page. The body tags must only be used once. The body tags are indented to make editing easier. **Body tags must be used after the closing head tag but before the closing html tag.**

Heading tags `</h1>` `</h1>`: the heading tag is similar to a paragraph heading. Using a heading tag will automatically make text a bold and larger font. There are six heading tags ranging from `<h1>` to `<h6>`. `<h1>` will display text using the largest font for main headings whilst `<h6>` will display text in a smaller font, often used for sub-headings.

Paragraph tags `<p>` `</p>`: identify the start and end of paragraphs. These are useful when you include a lot of text on a page. **The paragraph tag is placed within the body tag and below the heading tag.**

Bold tag < b > < /b > , *italic tag* < i > < /i > , or **underline tag** < u > < /u > should be placed on either side of the text to be formatted. These tags are opened and closed in the usual way.

Line break tags < br > insert a line break. There is no closing tag.

Colour tags use American spelling (color). The opening and closing colour tags are different. The opening tag < font color = red > or < font color = green > will change depending on what colour you are using but the closing tag < /font > remains the same.

In this chapter you are going to develop a web page about rainforests. The HTML code shown in this example uses tags to create a simple web page about rainforests.

In this example the web page is titled Rainforests. The body text includes headings in two different sizes. The largest heading < h1 > is Types of Rainforest. Temperate Rainforests is a smaller heading < h5 >.

You can use this example as a template when you design your own website. Do not expect your code to look exactly like the HTML in this example. You do not need to use colour when writing HTML. Colour has been used in this example to help your understanding.

```
< !DOCTYPE html >
< html >
< head >
    < title > Rainforests < /title >
< /head >
    < body >
        < h1 > Types of Rainforest < /h1 >
                Temperate < br >
                Tropical
        < h5 > Temperate Rainforests < /h5 >
                < p > Temperate rainforests are found along coastal regions
                in the temperate zone. < /p >
                < p > Temperate rainforests receive high rainfall. < /p >
    < /body >
< /html >
```

Using HTML tags to make a web page

⊕ Now you do it...

1 Make a folder in your work area titled: Web Page Revision

2 Open Notepad or another text editor.

3 Insert the simple elements needed to create a basic web page structure.

4 Add a few facts about rainforests or a topic of your choice.

5 Save your work as: revisionpage1.txt (saving your work in text format will let you return to the text version of your file for easy editing).

6 Save your work again, but this time change the document type to html. Click Save As and type as the file name: revisionpage1.html

🌐 If you have time...

↗ Use nesting to insert multiple tags on any piece of text. For example, use bold, italics or underline on a word of your choice.

📄 Test yourself...

1 What is a hyperlink and how is it used?

2 What is nesting?

3 How would you make the word 'Rainforest' green, bold and italic?

4 What is the difference between the head tag and a heading tag?

FACT

It can take many languages to make a website

Most websites are created by using more than one language. In addition to HTML, designers use CSS and Java as well as many more.

Key words

GUI: The Graphical User Interface (GUI) allows interaction with the computer using icons and menus rather than text.

HTML: HyperText Markup Language is used to build and create web pages.

Source code: Source code is a collection of commands or instructions used to create a program or to define a web page. When you view the source code of a web page you will be able to see the HTML, CSS, Java or other language that the web page is written in.

6.2 Plan your project

Learning outcomes

When you have completed this lesson you will be able to:

↗ plan the basic structure of a web page

↗ create the basic structure of a web page.

⌘ Learn about...

When planning a website you need to think about how the site will be structured. This will help you to check that pages flow in a logical order. A good plan will also save time when you start building your site.

You can plan the way your website will be structured by using a **site map**. A site map might be a diagram of your website or it might be text in the form of a list. Whether it is a diagram or list, your site map will show how the pages of your website link together.

You also need to think about how pages will link to each other and to the home page. You should also think about the overall design of your site.

Planning a website design

Remember from *Matrix 1*, Chapter 6, Creative Communications, that you can use a wireframe to plan the design of your web page. A **wireframe** helps you get an idea of how the website will look when it is finished. A wireframe is a simplified diagram of a web page that shows content, navigation and layout.

Content is the information presented on a web page. Content may be text, images, videos and music. A visitor will need to move from page to page on your website. The way a visitor moves around your website is called the navigation. The layout of a web page is the outline of where your headings, menus, images and content will go on your page.

The plan for your website should be more than just an outline. Your website plan should be detailed so that somebody else, such as a web designer, can follow your instructions and create your site. You should note font types, font size, colours and images. You should also include details of hyperlinks and information on how visitors will navigate the website.

Things to remember when designing a website

Audience

Your audience are the people who visit your website. Ask yourself who will use your website? What age are the visitors likely to be? Make sure visitors to your website can easily understand the language you use. Think about your audience when you decide which information to include and which colours to use. A good web page focuses on what your visitors will want to see, what colours they will like and the types of images they will find useful.

Content and purpose

When you have decided on your audience you can choose content. Remember, content is the information or images on your web page. Ask yourself if your website does what is supposed to do. Is the website for education, sales, communication or news or, perhaps, to share opinion?

The content of your website should be useful to your visitors. A good website has content that is accurate, relevant, reliable and focused.

The content you add to your website should be correct and factual, as this will make it accurate. You can make sure that you add reliable content by researching carefully and using sources you can trust. The content you add should also be up to date, as this will make it relevant. When you add content to a page, you should keep to your topic. This will make your content focussed. For example, when writing about the rainforest you should only mention facts about the rainforest and should not add information about the desert.

Navigation and layout

Websites should be easy to navigate. Visitors should be able to easily find what they are looking for. All hyperlinks should work and users should be able to get back to the home page quickly. Navigation should be consistent on every page. Consistent navigation means that the navigation menus will be in the same place on every page. Left or top navigation bars are often most useful. Using left or top navigation bars makes it easy for your visitor to find the link they are looking for. Give navigation buttons clear names so that users know exactly what to expect.

The layout should be clear, making the content easy to read. Balancing content and design features with white space is essential. Don't try to cram too much on one page. The layout on each page should be consistent and in keeping with a standard design. Keep graphics simple. If graphics are too big they will take a long time to load. Having to wait for an image to download could frustrate a visitor. Frustration might make a visitor want to leave your website.

Appearance

Keep the appearance simple, attractive and eye-catching. Visitors will decide if they like your site within a few seconds. Use colours and images that will appeal to your audience. For example, brighter colours and graphics are good for sites for children. An adult audience might prefer a simple and professional colour scheme.

There should be a good contrast between your background and your text.

Select just a few colours and use these consistently.

Selecting good colour combinations can be tricky, but there are many websites that can help you. Try sites like www.colrd.com or www.colorsontheweb.com to match colours to images and provide good range of colours.

⏻ How to...

You can sketch your site map by hand or you can use software tools such as Microsoft Word, Microsoft Visio, Creately or Gliffy.

We created the site map in this example using SmartArt in Microsoft Word. This site map is a hierarchy diagram. A hierarchy diagram shows items arranged by importance. This hierarchy diagram shows how our web pages are organised and how they link together. The Home page links to three other pages. The three other pages are called Type of Rainforest, Rainforest Animals and Rainfall.

To use SmartArt in Word, click Insert then SmartArt. Select Hierarchy. You can then select a hierarchy design of your choice. When you click a hierarchy design, you can edit the title of each box.

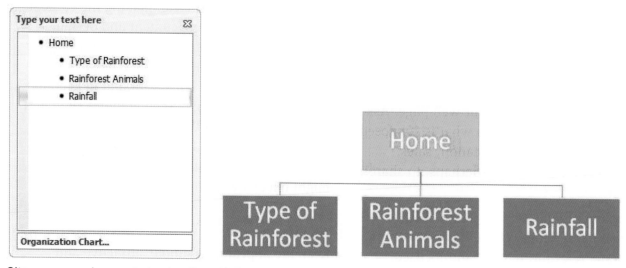

Site maps can be created using SmartArt

Creating a wireframe

There are many online templates to help you create a wireframe. Remember that you should be able to create a web page to match your wireframe. While you are learning the basics of web design, it is best to keep your wireframe simple. A sketch with details added is all you need to create simple websites. As your sites become more complex, you can start using a full wireframe.

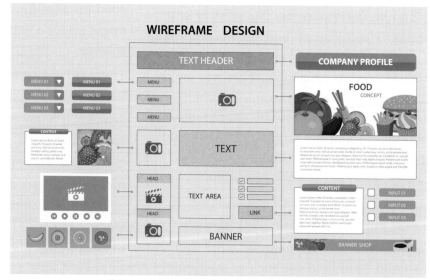

A wireframe and its completed design

This example shows a basic wireframe design. We created this design using text boxes in Microsoft Word. You can add detail such as font type, font size and colour to this sketch.

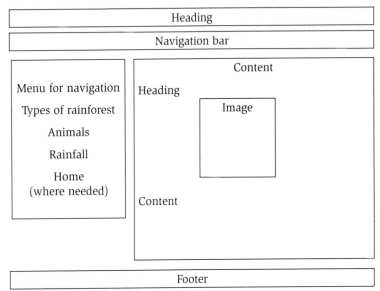

A basic wireframe design

 Now you do it...

By the end of this chapter, you will have created a website about the rainforest (or other topic chosen by your teacher).

This activity may take more than one lesson.

1   Plan your website and create a site map using a diagram.

2   Create a sketch or wireframe of your site. You should include a:
    - heading/title
    - simple left-hand navigation menu
    - space for content
    - place for an image
    - footer.

3   Add detail to your sketch to show, font colour, font type, background, image detail and any other information you think would be helpful to a design company.

 If you have time...

↗   Create your wireframe using software of your choice. Create the frame with the fonts and colours you intend to use on your web page.

Test yourself...

1   Identify four ways that content can be displayed on a website.
2   What is an advantage of using a wireframe?
3   Explain four features of a good website.
4   Explain the difference in colours and fonts that you might choose for an audience of children and an audience of adults when planning your website.

Key words

Site map: A site map shows the ordered structure and navigation of the individual pages in your website. A site map can be text in the form of a list or it can be a diagram.

Wireframe: A wireframe is a simplified diagram of a web page that shows content, navigation and layout.

Adding structure to your web page

Learning outcomes

When you have completed this lesson you will be able to:

↗ understand the difference between HTML and CSS

↗ identify reliable websites.

⌘ Learn about...

This lesson explains how to set up the layout of a web page. You will also research a topic so you can add content to your web page. This lesson will also help you to identify reliable websites for your research.

The difference between HTML and CSS

HTML gives a basic structure to a web page. To format a web page structure in a more advanced way, you can use **CSS** (Cascading Style Sheets).

CSS lets you create a style that you can use on different web pages. CSS gives you control over the layout of your web pages as well as the fonts, colours and backgrounds.

HTML and CSS work together to create attractive websites.

In this lesson you will meet a variety of HTML and CSS elements.

Style sheets

A **style sheet** describes how the web browser should display HTML elements on your web page. Style sheets created using CSS can be either internal or external.

An external style sheet is a CSS file that is stored separately to your web page. It allows you to control the way all the pages of a website look by editing this one file. You use an external style sheet when you want to apply the same style to many web pages.

An internal style sheet is included within an individual web page and controls the appearance of that page only. You use an internal style sheet when you want to apply a style to an individual page. Internal style sheets are added to the < head > section of a web page.

Investigating information online

The Internet is a great source of information but you need to be sure that the websites you use are accurate and reliable.

You should ask yourself:

↗ What do I know about the author of this website?

↗ Is the website up to date?

↗ Is the information **biased**?

Check the web address, especially the suffix (what the address ends in).

The most reliable websites are set up by official organisations that you can confirm.

Suffix	Description	Example
.co.uk	A UK-based company	http://www.bbc.co.uk
.ac	Usually an educational institution	http://www.ox.ac.uk
.com	Usually commercial organisations	http://www.apple.com
.org	A not for profit organisation	http://www.oxfam.org
.gov	A government organisation	https://www.gov.uk

 How to...

When you write CSS styles, you write your instructions in two parts. The first part is the selector and the second part is the declaration.

The selector shows the HTML element you want to style. For example, if you want to style a paragraph, then 'p' is the selector.

The declaration is the way you want an element to be styled. The declaration can be split into a property and a value. The property identifies exactly what you want to edit. For example, you might wish to edit the colour. The value shows what you want to change the colour to, for example, green.

When you write an instruction, start by writing the selector. Follow the selector with the declaration. The declaration should be written within curly brackets. You can use more than one declaration in each instruction. To close the declaration, use a semicolon (;) followed by a curly bracket.

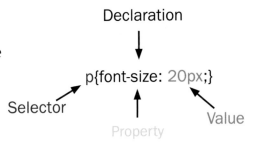

You can type the declaration on one line or, to make it easier to read, you can type each property on a separate line. In this example we are styling the paragraph in green with a font size of 20.

p{color:green; font-size: 20px;}   OR

p{
color:green;
font-size:20px;
}

Remember that CSS properties use American spellings. These CSS properties are useful:

- ↗ color: changes the colour of text
- ↗ font-size: changes the size of text
- ↗ font-weight: changes how heavy the font looks, for example bold
- ↗ font-style: changes the appearance of the font, for example italic
- ↗ font-family: changes the type of font, for example Arial, Impact or Courier
- ↗ text-transform: changes the case of text, for example uppercase, lowercase or capitalize (this makes each word start with a capital letter).

Add an internal style sheet

Internal style sheets are added into the < head > section on your HTML file. The tag used to add an internal style sheet is < style >. Remember to open and close the style tag. Anything in between the style tags is the CSS internal style code.

In this example, the internal style sheet has been made bold so you can easily identify it.

```
< !DOCTYPE html >

< html >

< head >

< title > Rainforests < /title >

    < style >

    h1{font-family:arial;text-transform:uppercase;font-
        size:40px;color:green}

    h2{font-family:arial;font-size:35px;color:green;font-style:italic}

    p{font-family:arial;font-size:25px;}

    < /style >

< /head >

    < body >

        < h1 > Types of Rainforest < /h1 >

        < h5 > Temperate Rainforests < /h5 >
```

 Now you do it...

Part A

1 Use websites that you can trust to explore the topic of rainforests.
2 Use word processing software to organise the information you have found. Write the name of the websites you have used and summarise the information you have read.

3 Add simple headings to your research. You can use these headings later as separate pages or headings on your website.

Part B

1 Make a folder in your work area titled Rainforest Website.

2 Open Notepad or another text editor.

3 Set up an HTML document as your home page.

4 Use your research to add:

  a a title

  b a heading

  c a sub-heading

  d one paragraph on your chosen topic.

5 Use HTML and CSS to format your home page. You can use the template from the 'How to…' section to help you.

6 Save your work as: homepage1.txt (Saving your work in the .txt format will let you return to the text version of your file for easy editing.)

7 Save your work again, but this time change the document type to html. Click Save As and type homepage1.html as the file name.

8 Test your home page by opening it in your web browser.

 If you have time...

✎ Open your web page using Microsoft Expression Web 4 or another web editor. Add a background colour and an image using the GUI (graphical user interface).

✎ Save your work as: HPextension.

Test yourself...

1 What does CSS stand for?

2 What CSS property would you use to change your font to lowercase?

3 Rewrite this on separate lines.

  h1{color:green; font-size: 20px;}

  Add an instruction to change the font to uppercase.

4 Write out the instruction to format a paragraph with:

  a blue font

  b Impact font

  c italic.

Key words

Bias: Bias is the tendancy of being one-sided.

CSS: CSS stands for Cascading Style Sheets. CSS is a style sheet language. CSS lets you create a style that you can use on multiple web pages.

Style sheet: A style sheet outlines how the browser should display HTML elements.

Learning outcomes

When you have completed this lesson you will be able to:

↗ understand margins, content, padding and borders

↗ understand and edit divisions and elements.

⌘ Learn about...

Every element that you add to a web page can have a box around it. Editing these boxes can give structure to your web page. Boxes can be set to any size. Boxes can be broken down into different parts:

↗ **Content:** This is where your text or image will appear.

↗ **Padding:** The area around the content. This area remains empty.

↗ **Border:** An area surrounding the padding and content.

↗ **Margin:** An area outside the border. This area remains empty.

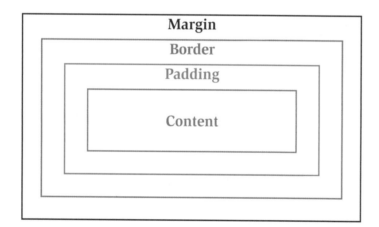

Using the div tag

A div tag < div > is used to create a division or define a section of your web page. Adding sections to your web page will let you style each section differently using CSS.

Div tags can be identified by adding a unique name to the div. This is useful for documents with several divisions. A div with a unique name is called a div id.

Using HTML layout tags

HTML 5 is the latest version of HTML. HTML 5 uses simple tags that add to the layout of your web page. You can use layout tags together with boxes. Using layout tags will add structure to your web page.

Tags used for layouts

- **Nav:** The nav tag identifies the main navigation area of your web page. The main navigation area can be a top-, right-, or left-aligned navigation bar.
- **Header:** The header tag should not be confused with head and heading tags (see Lesson 6.1). The head tag gives information about the web page. Heading tags identify paragraph headings on your page. The header tag is a layout element that can display the title of your web page.
- **Main:** The main tag shows where the main content of the web page will sit. Only use the main tag once per page.
- **Section:** The section tag shows a separate section of the web page.
- **Footer:** The footer tag identifies the footer of the web page.

⏻ How to...

You should have a basic web page that you created in Lesson 6.3. Your web page should show features such as paragraphs and titles. This lesson will show you how to add structure to your web page.

To add a div to your web page use the opening tag < div > and the closing tag < /div > .

When you have set the div you can now set a style to that division. You can also add a border to your div.

In this example, the div has a border of 3px and is solid green. Place the div description inside the style tag. The div tags should be placed in the body.

In a text editor the file would look like this.

```
< !DOCTYPE html >
< html >
< head >
< title > Rainforests < /title >
< style >
h1{font-family:arial;text-transform:uppercase;font-size:40px;color:green}
h2{font-family:arial;font-size:35px;color:green;font-style:italic}
p{font-family:arial;font-size:30px}
div {border:3px solid green}
< /style >
< /head >
    < body >
    < h1 > Types of Rainforest < /h1 >
    < h2 > Temperate Rainforests  < /h2 >
    < div > < p > Temperate rainforests are found along coastal regions in the
    temperate zone. < /p > < /div >
    < /body >
< /html >
```

This box shows the code as it would appear in a text editor. The code has been written in red to make it easy for you to identify. You do not need to add colour to your code for it to work.

161

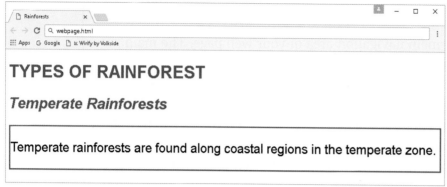

This is how the code looks in a web browser.

Add a div id

You can be more creative using a div id tag instead of a div tag. Using a div id tag, you can divide your web page into sections. You can then style each section differently.

Start adding div id tags from the top of a web page, working down to the bottom.

Div id tags work in a similar way to standard div tags. You must place the div description inside the style tag. The div id tags should be placed in the body. The div id tag needs to include a name of the div you are creating. Instead of using < div > to open the tag use < div id = "name" >. Close your div in the usual way using < /div >.

Adding a header tag

To create a div id for your title heading use:

< div id = "header" >

One you have assigned the div id to a section, you can set a style for that section.

When we refer to div id in the style section we use a hashtag #. For example, you can set the style for < div id = "header" > like this:

```
#header {background-color:grey;text-align:center;padding:10px;}
```

In this example, we set the background colour to grey and aligned the text to the centre. We also added padding of 10px. You can remove the padding if you wish. The box will just appear smaller.

Adding a nav tag

Adding a nav tag is a good way to create a navigation bar for your main hyperlinks.

Use #nav and < div id = "nav" > in the same way as you did for the header.

If you want your navigation to sit on the left side of your web page, you will also need to set the position of the box.

We typed each property on a separate line as we are editing more than one property.

```
#nav {
    background-color:grey;
    float:left;
    height:200px;
    width:150px;
    padding:10px;
}
```

In this example, we have set the navigation box with a grey background to match the header. You can set this to be any colour.

↗ Setting the float to the left will set the nav box on the left of the screen. You can change this to right if you want to.

↗ The height of the box from the top of the screen to the bottom is set at 200px. You can change this depending on how many navigation links you want to use in your box.

↗ The width of the box has been set to 150px. The width will depend on the size of your text going from left to right.

↗ The padding has been set to 10px. You can remove the padding if you wish.

Rainforest homepage: When you have completed your header, nav styles and tags, your web page should look something like this.

⊕ Now you do it...

1 Open the file homepage1.txt

2 Save this as homepage2.txt

3 Insert a div tag on the text of your choice.

3 Insert nav and header tags and styles. Your page should look similar to the Rainforest home page shown here.

🌐 If you have time...

↗ Copy the text from the file homepage2. Paste the text into Microsoft Expression Web 4 and edit the background colour.

↗ Save your work as HPextension2.

📄 Test yourself...

1 Identify the error in this style code:

h1{font-family:arial;text-transform:uppercase;font-size:40px;colour:green}

h2{font-family:arial;font-size:35px;colour:green;font-style:italic}

2 What is a div tag and when would you use it?

3 Explain the difference between the header, head and heading tags.

4 Write the code to style a header with a blue background, right-aligned text and padding of 20px.

Key words

Border: Border is an area surrounding the padding and content.

Content: Content is where your text or image will appear.

Margin: Margin is an area outside the border. This area remains empty.

Padding: Padding is the area around the content. This area remains empty.

6.5 Creating HTML links

Learning outcomes

When you have completed this lesson you will be able to:

↗ insert local and external hyperlinks

↗ insert a hyperlink to an email

↗ understand and edit attributes.

⌘ Learn about...

You can use HTML to create **hyperlinks** on your web page. When clicked, a hyperlink can take a visitor to a different part of your website. A link that takes you from one part of a website to another is known as known as a **local link**. A hyperlink can also take visitors to a different website. A link that takes you from one website to a different website is known as known as an **external link**.

You can add links by creating link tags. A link tag lets you create a hyperlink from text. Link tags are also called anchor tags or 'a tags'.

You can create a link from text, an image or a graphic, such as a button.

Email links

You can use HTML to create an email link. When a visitor to your website clicks an email link, a new email will open in their email software. The email will automatically be addressed with your email address.

Creating an email link makes it easy for a visitor to contact you.

 **How to...**

Create an external hyperlink

To turn text into a hyperlink we need to add a link tag around the text.
A hyperlink is defined by < a > < /a > tags.

After the opening tag you need to define the link address. Defining the link address gives more information about the address you are linking to. In this example we have used the attribute **href**.

An attribute gives extra information about an HTML element or tag. Attributes are always added in the opening tag.

In this example we have set **href** equal to

"http://www.google.com".

You must show the destination web page in double inverted commas.

We have made the text **Find out more** into a link that opens **http://www.google.com**.

By default the destination page opens in the window or tab that is currently in use. This means that your page will be replaced by the destination page. To make the destination page open in a new tab or window, you can add a target attribute to your code.

The target attribute says how the linked page should be opened. If you do not include a target, the page will open in the current window or tab. To make your page open in a new window or tab, add the attribute **target = _blank**.

< a href = "http://www.google.com" target = _blank > Find out more < /a >

Create a link to an internal page

When you link to an internal page, you only need to use the file name in your link. An internal page is part of your website. Remember to save all of your pages into one folder on your computer.

< a href = "tropicalrain.html" > Tropical < /a >

Create a link to an email

To create an email link, you also use the < a > tag. This link automatically opens a new email when you click it.

Destination address

< a href = "mailto:info@example.com" > Email me < /a >

The text to be displayed

You can also define other features of the email, such as the subject.

To set a subject you need to use **?subject =** after the email address. Remember to use double inverted commas. In this example, clicking the link **Email me** automatically opens an email addressed to **info@example.com** with the subject **Website Query**.

< a href = "mailto:info@example.com? subject = Website Query" > Email me < /a >

Create a link using an image

Hyperlinks can be created with text or graphics. To use an image as a hyperlink, first save the image in your working folder.

The tag used for images is **< img >**. The < img > tag does not need to be closed.

When adding an < img > tag, you also need to add the attribute **src**. Adding the attribute src identifies the source of the image. The attributes href and src work the same way.

This example is set in a new paragraph **< p >**. The paragraph contains the sentence 'Click here for more information'. This is followed by an image of a **plant**. When the user clicks the image, the website www.bbc.com will open. We have also specified the **size** of the image.

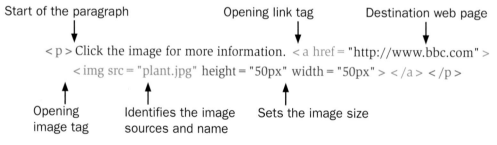

Start of the paragraph   Opening link tag   Destination web page

< p > Click the image for more information. < a href = "http://www.bbc.com" >
< img src = "plant.jpg" height = "50px" width = "50px" > < /a > < /p >

Opening image tag   Identifies the image sources and name   Sets the image size

It is sensible to add the attribute **alt** to an image link. Using alt shows alternative text when your image is not be displayed. It is important for visually impaired visitors to have access to alternative text. Adding alternative text allows the web browser to read out a description of the image. Although it is good to use alternative text, your image link will work without it.

< p > Click the image for more information. < a href = "http://www.bbc.com" >
< img src = "plant.jpg" alt = "plants" height = "50px" width = "50px" > < /a > < /p >

⊕ Now you do it...

Part A

1 Open the file homepage2.txt

2 Save this as homepage3.txt

3 Click File, Save As. Give your text file a new suitable name, for example Tropical Rain Forests.

4 Create a new page for your website. Use the research you gathered in Lesson 6.3. Do not edit the HTML or CSS. Edit the text only. This way the formatting will remain the same.

5 Save your work. Remember to keep all your website files in the same folder.

Part B

When your content is ready you can add these to your web page:

1 Insert a hyperlink to another web page in your website. This hyperlink could link your home page to your new page. For example, your Home page to Tropical Rain Forest.

2 Insert a hyperlink to an external website. You could link Home page to the BBC or other suitable web page.

3 Insert a link to an email. You could add a 'Contact Me' link on your home page.

4 Use an image as a hyperlink. You could add an image link to your second web page.

If you have time...

↗ Using the information you gathered in Lesson 6.3, create a new web page to go with your website. For example, if you have a page on tropical rainforests, you could create a page on temperate rainforests.

↗ Open your files in Microsoft Expression Web 4 and edit the site using the GUI.

Test yourself...

1 What is a link tag?

2 What is an attribute? Give an example.

3 What would you add to this code to make the destination page open in a new window?

   < a href = "http://www.google.com" > Find out more < /a >

4 Write out the code to link a web page to www.bbc.co.uk with hyperlink text that reads 'Click here for the BBC'.

Key words

External link: An external link is a hyperlink that links your web page to a web page on a different website.

Hyperlink: A hyperlink links one web page to another.

Local link: A local link is a hyperlink that links one page on your website to another page on your website.

Learning outcomes

When you have completed this lesson you will be able to:

↗ use data to create a graph

↗ save a graph as a web page

↗ analyse data and make a judgement.

Graphs and charts

Websites often contain data shown as graphs and charts. This lesson will show you how to create a graph in Microsoft Excel and add it to a web page. This lesson will focus on the three most commonly used graphs.

Types of graphs and charts

There are many types of graphs and charts that you can create using Microsoft Excel or other similar software. Using a graph or chart shows your data in a visual format. Graphs can make data easier to understand. The type of graph you choose depends on your aim and on the type of data you want to show.

You can make your graph easy to understand by labelling it clearly. All graphs should have a title and a key or legend. If your graph has axes, you should remember to label them. You should also show the units of measure being used.

The title is the heading used for a graph. A **key** identifies different types of data on a graph. A key is shown on the side or bottom of the graph. A key can also be called a legend.

Axes are the vertical and horizontal lines that surround a graph. Axes often have a scale. The scale is the relationship between the length of the axis and what it represents, and that can include the units of measure used.

Pie charts

Pie charts show how individual items add up to make a whole. A pie chart shows proportions of each item. If you add the portions together the total is 100 per cent.

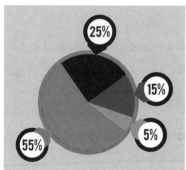

Bar charts

Bar charts are useful for making comparisons between two or more values. The bars can be vertical or horizontal. A bar chart with vertical bars is sometimes called a column chart.

If the bars are vertical, the horizontal axis (across the bottom) normally shows the item that you are plotting. For example, you can plot the amount of rainfall each month. The vertical axis (on the left side) shows values linked with each item, for example, millimetres.

Line graphs

Line graphs are useful for showing changes over a period of time and for spotting a **trend** or pattern.

 How to...

You can create a graph using Microsoft Excel.

1 Open Microsoft Excel.

2 In cell A1, type a suitable heading for your spreadsheet.

3 Add the data you want to analyse. Arrange your data in columns.

4 Highlight the data you want to use.

5 Click Insert and select Chart. Choose a chart type.

6 Save your work.

7 You can edit your title by right-clicking the title and selecting Format Chart Title. You can also do this using the Chart Title icon.

8 Select Layout from the Chart Tools menu. Then select Axis Titles and label your axes.

9 You can also use this menu to edit your titles and other features.

10 Right-click the edge of the chart and move your chart to a new sheet.

11 Type over the default name 'Chart 1' to give your new sheet a name.

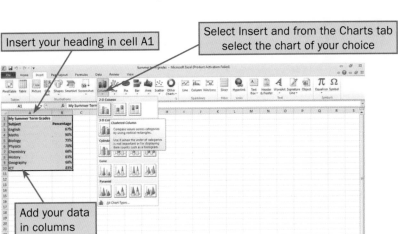

Insert your heading in cell A1

Select Insert and from the Charts tab select the chart of your choice

Add your data in columns

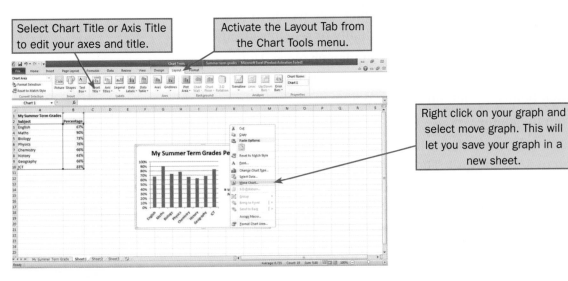

Select Chart Title or Axis Title to edit your axes and title.

Activate the Layout Tab from the Chart Tools menu.

Right click on your graph and select move graph. This will let you save your graph in a new sheet.

12 Right-click the graph and select Format Data Series. Change the colour and appearance of your graph.

13 Click File, Save As and save your work.

14 Click File and Save As again and save your graph as a web page.

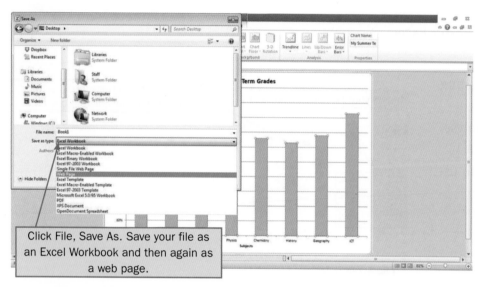

Click File, Save As. Save your file as an Excel Workbook and then again as a web page.

Describe your graph

When you have a graph, you can use it to see any trends or differences in your data.

When you analyse your graph you can:

1 Look for patterns from left to right.

2 Describe the pattern by referring to the axes. Key words to use when describing a pattern are: increase, decrease, rise, fall or remain steady.

3 Describe the pace at which the graph is changing. Key words to use when describing pace are: slowly, fast, sharply, gradually or remains steady.

4 Identify anything unusual. Take note of any sudden changes. Notice high or low points on the graph. Key words to use when describing a graph are: maximum for high points, minimum for low points.

5 Refer to data from the graph.

An example of a good analysis is: The temperature increases slowly from 30°C in January to a high of 35°C in April. The temperature drops quite sharply to 29°C in May. The temperature continues to drop gradually each month to a minimum of 15°C in October. In November the temperature slowly starts climbing again.

Now you do it...

1 Using a source you can trust, investigate data on rainfall or temperatures in the rainforest.

2 Type this data into Microsoft Excel or other software.

3 Create a graph based on this data.

4 Save the graph as a web page.

5 Open your Rainforest website using Microsoft Expression Web 4.

6 Add a new page to your website.

7 Add an appropriate title and sub-heading.

8 Write a paragraph about your graph, describing any patterns you have found.

9 Add a hyperlink to this page that will open the graph you have created and saved as a web page. See Lesson 6.5 to remind you how to do this in HTML. You can also use the GUI to link your pages together. To use the GUI, right-click on the text you want to link and select Hyperlink. Follow the wizard to help you.

 If you have time...

↗ Find an online video about the rainforest. You can use a website such as YouTube.

↗ Add a link to this video to your website. You can use the GUI to do this.

 Test yourself...

1 When would it be best to use a bar chart as a way of showing data?

2 When plotting data such as temperature that changes over time, would you use a line or bar graph? Why would you choose this type of graph?

3 What four things should you add to a bar or line graph to make it clear and easy to read?

4 Give four examples of things you might consider when analysing a graph.

Key words

Axes: Axes are the vertical and horizontal lines that surround a graph.

Key: A key identifies different types of data on a graph.

Trend: A trend is a pattern seen on a graph.

Review what you have learned about creative communication

Overview

In this chapter you have learned how to:

- use HTML to edit or create a basic web pages
- plan and create the basic structure of a web page
- understand the difference between HTML and CSS
- identify reliable websites
- add a simple left-hand menu to a web page
- understand margins, content, padding and borders
- understand and edit divisions, elements and attributes
- insert local and external hyperlinks
- insert a hyperlink to an email
- use text and images as a hyperlink
- use data to create a graph
- save a graph as a web page
- analyse data and make a judgement.

 ## Test questions

1. What does CSS stand for?
2. What HTML tag is used to define an internal style sheet?
3. Name the CSS property that is used to change the size of text.
4. What HTML tag do you use to create a line break?
5. What does text-transform do?
6. Explain the difference between < h1 >, < head > and < header >.
7. What does the attribute href do?
8. What suffix is often used at the end of a university web page?
9. Explain the difference between a bar chart and a pie chart.
10. What two things could you look at to try to identify a trend?

 ## Assessment activities

Starter activity

- Create a new folder called Assessment2 in your work area.
- Open a text editor and create a new web page called Assessment2.
- Type in the code shown here.
- Correct three mistakes in the code.
- Add the missing line break.
- Save and close your file.

```
< !DOCTYPE html >

< html >

< head >

    < title >  Rainforests  < /title >

< /head >

        < h1 > Types of Rainforest  < /h1 >

                Temperate

                Tropical

        < h5 > Temperate Rainforests

            < p >  Temperate rainforests are found along coastal
            regions in the temperate zone.  < /p >

            < p >  Temperate rainforests receive high rainfall.  < p >
```

Intermediate activity

↗ Open the file called Assessment2.
↗ Add an internal style sheet to format the heading < h5 > . Change the font
  colour to blue.
↗ Save and close your page.

Extension activity

↗ Open the file called Assessment 2.
↗ Add an email link to the page. Your link should allow a user to send you an
  email after clicking the text, Contact Me.
↗ Save and close your file.

Index